Chp 1-2 (Jan 31)
3-8, (Feb 7)
12-13
14-16 (Feb 14) + Bible
17-18 (Feb 16)
10-11 (Mar 21)
19 (Apr 18)

MISSIO
·DEI·

MISSIO
•DEI•
A *W*ESLEYAN *U*NDERSTANDING

EDITED BY

KEITH SCHWANZ *and* JOSEPH COLESON

BEACON HILL PRESS
OF KANSAS CITY

Copyright 2011 by Beacon Hill Press of Kansas City

ISBN 978-0-8341-2717-3

Printed in the
United States of America

Cover Design: J.R. Caines
Internal Design: Sharon Page

Scripture quotations marked KJV are from the King James Version of the Bible.

Scripture quotations from the following versions are used by permission:

The *Holy Bible, New International Version*® (NIV®). Copyright © 1973, 1978, 1984 by Biblica, Inc.™ Used by permission of Zondervan. All rights reserved worldwide. www.zondervan.com.

The *New King James Version* (NKJV). Copyright © 1982 by Thomas Nelson, Inc. All rights reserved.

The *New Revised Standard Version* (NRSV) of the Bible, copyright 1989 by the Division of Christian Education of the National Council of the Churches of Christ in the USA. All rights reserved.

The *Holy Bible, Today's New International Version*™ (TNIV®). Copyright © 2001, 2005 by International Bible Society. All rights reserved worldwide.

Library of Congress Cataloging-in-Publication Data

Missio Dei : a Wesleyan understanding / edited by Keith Schwanz and Joseph Coleson.
    p. cm.
   Includes bibliographical references.
   ISBN 978-0-8341-2717-3 (pbk.)
  1. Mission of the church. 2. Church of the Nazarene—Doctrines. I. Schwanz, Keith. II. Coleson, Joseph E., 1947-
   BV601.8.M58 2011
   262'.7—dc22

                      2010049509

10 9 8 7 6 5 4 3 2 1

CONTENTS

FOREWORD

In recent years I have longed for a word that would challenge the confusion and uncertainty that seems to pervade much of the Church of Jesus Christ at the present time. Tension and ambiguity seem to characterize the conversations that are occurring, and we often are at odds with one another without being able to fully articulate why.

In reading through the manuscript for this book, I began to have hope. Here is a different and better way to approach the conversation. Here is careful, reflective, and articulate expression of the reason why we should be "a missional church." We have a missional God!

As some have said in recent months, "It is not so true that the church has a mission, as it is true that the mission has a church." This is the point of our work. This is not a humanly devised agenda. The work of mission is the nature and character of God. From the beginning of creation, through the establishment of the people of Israel, through the Exodus, the Promised Land, the periods in exile, to the Incarnation, Calvary, and Pentecost, God is a seeking God!

As the people of God we are to be engaged in the mission of God! The work of the church is to engage in that mission carefully, reflectively, and with profound intention.

It is a generous gift to the body of Christ, that the faculty of Nazarene Theological Seminary has provided us with this magnificent resource. The essays are thoughtful, theologically sound, and unambiguous. Mission is not an option for the church. It is in the very character of the relationship we as a people, as well as individuals, have with a missional God. God's passion is to be the motive and power of our mission.

I commend this book to every pastor, superintendent, evangelist, and layperson. Here is a resource for our thinking, our planning, and our doing. While it is not a "how-to" book, it is most definitely a "why" book. Once you begin to pore over these essays, you will begin to ask more appropriate questions of your planning. This will challenge some of our untested assumptions and will cause us to rethink some of our methods. But it will also give us a solid footing on which to move forward in this vital, necessary, and compelling work of the church.

Jesse C. Middendorf
General Superintendent, Church of the Nazarene

PREFACE

Many people try to make sense of the dramatic changes in our world. Some hope this is just another generational adjustment. Countless people, however, are convinced the rumblings indicate a seismic cultural shift. Some refer to the massive realignment as "rapid, discontinuous change." The rate of change is very fast. It doesn't seem to fit with what came before.

People once convinced that social problems could be eradicated through education no longer believe those claims. The issues seem to be more complex than what the human mind can comprehend or society has the will to confront. They no longer trust the tendency to reduce multifaceted matters to a few bullet points in a presentation. Life is just too messy for that. People question authority after being deeply disappointed by civic and religious leaders. A pervasive cynicism clouds the perception of many. Those who have been in the church for decades recognize the loss of respect for Christianity. The Christian church no longer has favored status in an increasing number of places.

Sometimes the word "liminality"—the Latin root means "threshold"—is used to describe the state of the transition we are experiencing. We are in a liminal period; the old is being abandoned and the new is emerging. In the midst of profound change, we cannot yet see clearly what lies ahead. We instinctively long for clarity as we gaze into the future, but find ourselves staring through a gauze of ambiguity instead.

Church leaders ponder what these cultural changes mean for congregations and denominations. Pastors wonder why they seem less effective than they were twenty-five years before. People beyond the church no longer pay attention to a congregation's outreach programs. What does the church do in light of the massive movement in cultural norms?

In the early years of the twenty-first century, some church leaders began using the term "emerging church." An avalanche of books provided preliminary attempts to chart for the church the implications of the massive changes society was experiencing. But there is an older and broader discussion about the church's response to cataclysmic change: the missional church.

MISSIO DEI, MISSIONAL CHURCH

Lesslie Newbigin's name often appears in the missional church conversation. The Church of Scotland sent Newbigin to India in 1936 as a missionary. Newbigin eventually became a bishop in the ecumenical Church of South India. He applied what he had learned from his missionary experience to the post-modern context he found in his homeland when he retired to England in 1974.

Newbigin challenged Christians in the West to consider a new paradigm. He began to speak of Christians being sent by God instead of by the institutional church. God initiated the mission, he said. The reign of God does not rest on human ingenuity or initiative. Newbigin understood the *missio Dei* in a Trinitarian construct: proclaiming the reign of God, sharing in the life of Jesus, empowered by the Spirit. The role of the Christian, then, must be to discern what God is doing and get involved.

The Gospel and Our Culture Network developed in the 1990s to explore what it means to be the missional church in North America. Writers such as Lois Barrett, Darrell Guder, and George Hunsberger provided influential books.

The Lausanne Committee for World Evangelization sponsored the 2004 Forum for World Evangelization in Pattaya, Thailand. Out of this gathering came Lausanne Occasional Paper Number 39, "The Local Church in Mission: Becoming a Missional Congregation in the Twenty-first Century Global Context." The missional church conversation was no longer limited to the West. Representatives from the global Christian community now described the responsibilities of the church as missional.

Very quickly the use of the word "missional" increased. Some complained it was not a legitimate word because they could not find it in a dictionary. Others quickly adopted the word since it seemed to have a fresh, creative sound to it. John Dally noted how some co-opted the word: "There is a rush today to rebaptize everything 'missional.' . . . Many 'missional' churches are using the word to describe more familiar activities . . . but they leave the institutional church very much intact and postpone for a later day reflection on the nature of God and the pattern of God's activity in the world."[1]

A review of several "best practices" books that have "missional" in the title revealed a strange absence of theological reflection. Instead, the books list techniques and tricks on how to get more people inside the doors of the church. The authors used the word "missional" on the cover but focused on getting the "world" to come to church instead of the church going to the world. "They also overlook the fact that at the very heart of the sea change represented by the reemergence of missionality is the claim that it is God who is missional, not the church. The church can become missional only by reflecting God's missional nature, not by introducing new programs or sending invitational fliers to potential new members."[2] In the spirit of Newbigin, Guder, and others, Dally suggested that any conversation about the missional church must find its motivation in theological reflection.

That's where this book joins the missional church conversation. In *Missio Dei,* the faculty of Nazarene Theological Seminary guides theological reflection to further the understanding of and participation in God's mission. If the practices of the church are not motivated by a white-hot core of theological convictions, the church will rush from fad to fad in search of the next "cool" idea. By contrast, if the practices of the church emerge from deeply held theological convictions, the church will remain centered on God and God's purposes.

The subtitle is important too; the book is *Missio Dei: A Wesleyan Understanding.* We write as persons who have benefited from a Wesleyan heritage. We find deep resonance between Wesleyan theology and the missional church discussion. For example, what the missional church literature describes as God's initiative in seeking to redeem the world is understood as prevenient grace from a Wesleyan theological perspective. God's preceding grace draws persons to God. Further, Wesleyans believe God offers the invitation to all through the unlimited atonement. Christ died for all, and all who receive God's gift through faith are being saved. Consider these stanzas by Charles Wesley as an illustration of the Wesleyan understanding of prevenient grace and the unlimited atonement:

Come, sinners, to the Gospel feast;
Let every soul be Jesus' guest.
Ye need not one be left behind,
For God hath bid all humankind.

Sent by my Lord, on you I call;
The invitation is to all.
Come, all the world! Come, sinner, thou!
All things in Christ are ready now.[3]

Since God is already at work through prevenient grace, the church's role is to participate in God's mission already begun. God's desire is that every person be made spiritually alive through faith in Jesus. The church, then, must extend God's reconciliation to all with whom it has contact. All is sacred; that is, all is of concern to God. The wall between the sacred and the secular is broken down because of prevenient grace.

MARKS OF A MISSIONAL CHURCH

Pastor Mark stepped to the microphone and greeted the congregation gathered for worship. Then he surprised them by asking that they take their Bibles and turn to Galatians 2. Most Sundays they sang first, but not this week.

Mark began to speak as the rustling of pages subsided. "In Galatians 2 we read about Paul confronting Peter who had huddled up with his Jewish friends. They ignored the Gentile Christians and did their own thing in the back corner. When you get down to verse 14 you see that Paul says they were out of alignment with the gospel. Their exclusionary actions didn't line up with what Jesus taught or how Jesus lived."

Mark paused for a moment. He made eye contact with several in the congregation. "As I've pondered this passage this week," Mark continued, "I started wondering if Paul would find us in alignment with the gospel. I *think* so. We've got some good things going on these days. But just to be sure we understand God's design for us, we've got a plan to help us be doers of the Word this morning."

Mark called Hannah and Molly to the front. Hannah described how the workers in the senior adult care facility across the street from the church would be expecting them in fifteen minutes. A manager would meet them inside the main door and would give them cards, each with the name and room number of a resident. "Let the manager know," Hannah said, "if you would be willing to visit with people in the Alzheimer's unit. She'll give you instructions on how to get into the secured area."

Then Molly stepped to the mic to talk about arrangements for lunch. "Take as long as you want. When you are done at the care facility, come back to the church. We'll have soup and sandwiches ready for lunch."

As Hannah and Molly returned to their seats, Mark invited the people to pray. Several members of the congregation led in sentence prayers. They asked God to use them to share love and grace with the senior adults. A quiet, holy energy came upon the congregation.

When they finished the prayer, Mark asked the congregation to stand to receive a blessing. "'May the grace of the Lord Jesus Christ, and the love of God, and the fellowship of the Holy Spirit be with you all' [2 Cor 13:14, TNIV]. May your words of encouragement and acts of kindness be in line with the gospel." Several in the congregation said, "Amen," in response to the blessing.

A conversational buzz started as people gathered their things to head out to the care facility. A grandfather and grandson decided to be a team. A young couple invited a college student to join them. "Oh, yeah, I almost forgot," Mark called out over the talking. "The ushers will be at the door to receive your tithes and offerings." A pleasant laughter bubbled through the sanctuary at the announcement.

A missional community comes to life when a theologically formed, gospel-centered, Spirit-empowered fellowship of Jesus followers embodies the redemptive mission of God.

The missional community begins in the redemptive mission of God. It has no other reason for existence. The generative life of the community comes as the people participate in the ongoing mission of God. The missional fellowship embodies the gospel both in its proclamation and actions; it *shows* and *tells* the good news. The community is formed by its reflection on the character and nature of God, centered on the eternal reign of Jesus, and empowered by the Holy Spirit.

The redemptive mission of God includes the community of Jesus followers being called and gathered, centered, and sent.

The missional church is ***called and gathered.***

- The missional church knows its life flows from the triune God who called it into existence.
- The missional church gathers as the people of God whose shared life witnesses to God's redemptive mission.
- The missional church shares the responsibilities of servant leadership.

The missional church is ***centered.***

- The missional church centers itself in the *missio Dei* by learning to live in the way of Jesus through worship and discipleship.
- The missional church seeks to be recreated in the *imago Dei* so as to be holy in heart and life.
- The missional church discerns the *missio Dei* through biblical and theological reflection on its practices and sent-ness.

The missional church is ***sent.***

- The missional church orients itself as being sent by God to embody the *missio Dei.*
- The missional church nurtures redemptive relationships through hospitality, generosity, compassion, and witness.
- The missional church lives the cruciform life through incarnational presence and self-emptying service for the sake of the world.

The missional community finds its identity as the called and gathered, centered, and sent people of God. It also establishes a rhythm of missional living that carries it from day to week to year, both as a community and as individuals. Daily they intentionally seek to embody the ministry of reconciliation that they have received from God. When they gather for weekly worship they enact the gospel through the renewal of their commitment to the Lord Jesus Christ. They celebrate the life of Jesus throughout the year and are spiritually formed by the very gospel they proclaim. The rhythm of missional living carries the missional community to greater faithfulness to God and effectiveness as participants in God's mission.

MISSIO DEI: A WESLEYAN UNDERSTANDING

This book is part of the ***reVisioning* NTS** project supported by a grant from the Kern Family Foundation. Our peers in the "Leading Through Change: Innovation in Theological Schools" encouraged us to clarify how our proposal to be a "missional seminary serving a missional church" emerged from our theological convictions. We added this book to our project in response to our peers in the Kern grant program. The primary objective of this book is to provide a theological rationale for the character and practices of the missional church.

The book begins with an overview of the missional church and introduces issues central to the discussion. In chapter 1, David Wesley, associate professor of Intercultural Studies, states that the church *is* the missionary. The church is *not* the mechanism that sustains a missions program.

Part 1

Part 1 traces the *missio Dei* in the Bible, both the Old and the New Testaments.

- In chapter 2, Joseph Coleson, professor of Old Testament, maintains that God's mission in creation was to form humans capable of relationship with God.
- In chapter 3, Roger Hahn, professor of New Testament, argues that God's mission reaches to the whole world. God initiated a covenant with Abraham through whom to form a holy nation in order to bring reconciliation to the world.
- In chapter 4, Joseph Coleson explores how the prophets called Israel to return to God's mission, especially concerning justice for the poor and powerless.
- In chapter 5, Roger Hahn describes Jesus' articulation of God's mission in the kingdom of God passages found in the Gospels.
- In chapter 6, Andy Johnson, professor of New Testament, says that the church functions as God's "display people" to reveal that God's reign has begun.

Part 2

Part 2 provides a Wesleyan theology of the *missio Dei*.

- In chapter 7, Thomas Noble, professor of theology, explains that the triune God is both a sending God and a sent God. The church has no mission of its own but participates in God's mission.
- In chapter 8, Thomas Noble explains that Jesus was sent not only to preach, teach, and heal but also to empty himself to the point of death. Likewise, all who would participate in God's mission must take up the cross and follow Jesus.
- In chapter 9, Steve McCormick, professor of historical theology, explains that through the Holy Spirit the people of God have been "re-membered" into the body of Christ. Through the Holy Spirit they "embody" the mission of God.
- In chapter 10, Steve McCormick claims that the church cannot *be* the church apart from mission. Through a new way of *being*, the body of Christ reflects God's nature and mission.
- In chapter 11, Ron Benefiel, president of Nazarene Theological Seminary, discusses the fact that the kingdom of God is both here now, but also not yet. The church is a living illustration of what the kingdom will look like when Jesus returns.
- In chapter 12, Brent Peterson, associate professor of theology at Northwest Nazarene University, explains that the church witnesses to God's redemption in this time and place.
- In chapter 13, William Selvidge, associate professor of intercultural studies, explores some of the ramifications of God's offer of redemption to the *whole* world. Since this is so, the missional church participates in God's mission amid people in all cultures.

Part 3

Part 3 explores some of the ways we participate in the *missio Dei*.

- In chapter 14, Keith Schwanz, assistant dean and lecturer in church music, proposes that worship involves telling God's story. The church proclaims God's story in the weekly corporate worship and embodies God's story in a daily lifestyle.
- In chapter 15, Dean Blevins, professor of Christian education, portrays discipleship as spiritual formation and missional engagement working together. As we are transformed by God, we become transformational agents in the world.

- In chapter 16, Judith Schwanz, professor of pastoral care and counseling, explains that God calls the church to a shared life. The church does not face inward, but through a shared-out life makes room for those beyond the church.
- In chapter 17, Harold Raser, professor of the history of Christianity, delves into compassionate ministry as an expression of God's care for the world.
- In chapter 18, Lyle Pointer, adjunct professor of evangelism, describes the church's witness as a means of God's grace. This involves an incarnational presence, redemptive conversations, compassionate care, and an inclusive community.
- In chapter 19, Douglas Hardy, professor of spiritual formation, claims that what was formed at the creation of the world is deformed while living in the world. But what was deformed can be reformed to enable living *for* the world.

OUR THANKS AND OUR PRAYER

Nazarene Theological Seminary expresses its deepest appreciation to Dr. Patricia E. Kern, Dr. Robert D. Kern, and the Kern Family Foundation for their support of the **reVISIONing NTS** project. The financial support of the Kern Family Foundation has allowed NTS to explore more deeply what it means to be a "missional seminary serving a missional church."

Those of us who have worked on this project for more than a year now offer the book to the church. We pray that it may fan into flame the gifts and passions of God's people so that the reign of God will be known on earth as it is in heaven.

Keith Schwanz

1

THE CHURCH AS MISSIONARY
David Wesley

═══════════════════════ ◆ ═══════════════════════

As a missionary in South America, I worked with a team of leaders who often wrestled with the changing nature of the church and the nature of God's mission. For some time, missionaries had noticed a "disease" that seemed to take over and destroy those churches that focused on the church building as the center of mission, and that thought the goal of the church was to attract people to come to church. We called this disease *templismo,* to represent a congregation that focuses on the building. We discovered the cure for this disease was for a congregation to turn inside out and focus on what God was doing in their community, to build relationships with friends who were not Christians, and to pray for them daily.

During that time I also began to discover authors such as David Bosch who articulated some of these same issues. When I came to the U.S. in 2005 to teach at Nazarene Theological Seminary, I found myself drawn particularly to the writings of Lesslie Newbigin, who also expressed forcefully the need for congregations in the West to learn the culture around them, instead of only trying to attract people into the church building. My current reading includes Darrell Guder and others who are developing a network of individuals writing about God, God's mission, and the church as responding to God's mission.

Now, the teaching faculty at NTS also has begun to join this conversation, as Wesleyan theologians and scholars. This ongoing conversation challenges all of us to explore and to affirm the very core of our identity as Christians of the Wesleyan tradition. For Christians infected with *templismo,* this way of thinking can seem threatening. It is, after all, a call to holiness that moves us to follow God's radical mission, a mission that destroys idols. This way of thinking also moves us outward to listen to, to love, and to engage a complex world, and that can be daunting.

A CHANGING WORLD

World culture has changed drastically in recent history, and mission looks quite different than it did just a few years ago. Several authors have described a phenomenon in which the mission efforts of the colonialist past, which involved enormous sacrifice, have now come full circle. The prayers, sacrificial giving, and investments of missionary lives have resulted in a movement of Christianity—not in Europe or the United States, but rather in Africa, Latin America, and Asia. So great is this movement that many in the West have begun to look to places such as Africa (formerly considered "deep, dark Africa") for direction, to help the West experience similar growth and spiritual vitality.

A couple of years ago, I attended a meeting with a group of Christians just returned from the Horn of Africa. Earlier generations had traveled to Africa to spend their lives there as professional missionaries. Now, by contrast, a group of volunteers had visited East Africa with one simple objective: to learn *from* Africans how to live an intentional Christian lifestyle.

I was encouraged by the reports of the group members. They understood that Christians in the West have much to learn from missional Christians in other parts of the world, such as Africa. I listened as they told about pastors and laypeople risking their lives to share their faith. We were all awed at how God was transforming so many lives.

"We long to see the same thing happen in the U.S.," one person said, and I was thrilled to hear this. But then he continued, "We noticed how the Africans organize in small groups and follow certain practices. We believe these practices are the reason they are having the growth we desire in the U.S." He then proposed a plan by which the same structures could be implemented in the U.S., in hopes of seeing the same results.

I wasn't sure if I should cry or laugh. Church growth techniques are not the primary thing we should learn from Christians in Africa, nor are large numbers of converts the best indicator of a missional church. The greatest lesson the West can learn is how to deepen our Christian walk, and how to be dependent on God, rather than on programs and strategies. The reason for the great movement in the Horn of Africa is not a strategy or program, but their desperation for God. They know they need God, and they know they must be part of what God is doing. Some in that part of the world describe this as "having the DNA of God." I would call it "being missional." When people become this dependent on God, they draw near to him in worship. Then they realize the very heartbeat or passion of God is mission. Such people know that being in relationship with God means sharing in his nature and sharing in his passion.

When the expansion of Christianity, and the resulting worldwide interconnectedness that recent authors have described as globalization, merge with a theological emphasis known as missional theology, it heralds a new and exciting day for the church to be the body of Christ.

MISSION, MISSIONARY, AND THE *MISSIO DEI*

Words and phrases convey concepts. Moreover, old words fade or change or add meanings and nuances, and new words emerge. To avoid confusion, we have to pay attention to the changes.

Mission

Mission is the most identifiable aspect of the body of Christ. Mission is not a program or plan of the church; neither is it a slogan or mission statement that gives administrative direction. Mission is the very nature of the church, seeking first God and his kingdom. It flows directly from God. A living relationship with the God of mission distinguishes the church as a living organism, as opposed to a mechanistic (and secular) organization. Because of this relationship, we truly can say that the church does not *support* a program of missions; rather, the church *is* the missionary.

Missionary

Few words have changed more in recent history than the word "missionary." Currently, "missionary" is open to a range of definitions and interpretations. On one end of the spectrum, uninformed media coverage and some popular novels portray missionaries as colonialist destroyers of local culture. There is just enough truth in this portrayal that "missionary" is not a positive term in many parts of the world. (It is also true that missionaries have promoted and helped to preserve many indigenous cultures through reducing languages to writing, through translation, and by various other means.)

At the other end of the spectrum, some use the term "missionary" to define any Christian who does anything in any part of the world for any reason. A third perspective defines a missionary in professional terms. The *Manual* of the Church of the Nazarene, for example, defines a missionary merely as "a member of the clergy or a layperson who has been appointed by the General Board to minister for the church."[1] Such a variety of definitions underscores our need to develop a clear understanding of mission as *God's* mission, if we are to find a way forward.

The *Missio Dei*

The Church of the Nazarene is working to clarify an understanding of the missional church and missional theology that remains true to Scripture as well as true to its theological identity within the larger Christian body. In 1984, Nazarene missiologist Paul Orjala wrote a simple missionary book, titled *God's Mission Is My Mission,* addressing themes that had surfaced in mission conferences sponsored by the World Council of Churches since 1952. Academic scholars and writers such as David Bosch and Lesslie Newbigin had discussed these themes and wrestled with the need for the West to see mission in new and different ways. For the most part, however, this had remained an academic discussion, not yet popularized in the broader Christian church or the Church of the Nazarene. While Orjala did not develop a missional theology in this missionary reading book, he did establish a basis for understanding mission as being, first and foremost, *God's* mission. The term he and others used for this understanding was *missio Dei,* a Latin term for "God's mission."

The groundbreaking idea behind "God's mission" rests in the understanding that mission always has its source in God. Missiologist David Bosch asserted that "mission" defines God's nature. Mission is not a program of the church that we do on special Sundays or highlight occasionally at district mission events. In every part of the Bible, from Genesis to Revelation, Scripture makes it clear that God is a missionary God. God's love for "the nations," and God's desire for his people to share in his passion, is never a secondary issue. This missional love stands at the very center of who God is and who God expects the church to be.

In the New Testament record, we read of the church sending apostles to people of varied ethnic backgrounds. The church, however, did not limit mission to a congregational program of sending missionaries to "the ends of the earth." The church didn't just *have* missionaries; the church itself *was* the missionary in Jerusalem, Judea, and Samaria, as well as to the ends of the earth. Another way to state this perspective is to say that the church is not just a sending church; it also is a *sent* church. This statement has enormous implications.   Sending + Sent
(saving)   (saved)

THE MISSIONAL CHURCH

It is necessary here to take a brief detour, if we would understand the complexity of our task, and acknowledge that the greatest challenge is the pervasive consumerism within the church. For the past twenty years, nearly all church "strategies" have focused on a "seeker" mentality, which is consumer driven. The seeker church begins with a marketing approach to determine the "target" audience's needs and desires, and then constructs church services and programs to meet those needs. This technique, though effective in attracting some into the church, is highly individualistic and too easily becomes a business of selling religious "goods and services." This way of viewing the church begins with humanity at the center, and consumer-oriented programs, promoted during church services, become the central focus of missions.

The missional church, on the other hand, begins with the idea that mission is God's nature and God's activity (the *missio Dei*) and, furthermore, that the church is the missionary. By definition, the church is the *sent* church. The "business" of the church, then, is to train missionaries to *go* and to live out the gospel in their spheres of influence. The missional church, therefore, does not shape programs around consumerist Christian desires. The missional church designs ministries that equip people to show the gospel to the nonbeliever. This is not done as a program but as a lifestyle.

Missionary Lesslie Newbigin provides a great example of the sent church. Newbigin served as a missionary in India and developed a plan for building the church, educating leaders, and developing churches as sent communities. When Newbigin would confirm and receive people into full communion with the church, he would announce: "Now you are the Body of Christ in this village. You are God's apostles here. Through you they are to be saved. I will be in touch with you. I will pray for you. I will visit you. If you want my help I will try to help you. But *you* are now the mission."[2] Newbigin commented that when this statement was made from the first day onward—that being a Christian community is about living as a sent community—then the gospel would spread. If one denies this responsibility to the young church, then it does the church irreparable harm.

Newbigin's paradigm demonstrates more than his concern about local participation in mission. The paradigm reveals that he was also concerned with participation in mission "to the ends of the earth." Newbigin did not see mission as something done just by churches from one part of the globe, or when a church was large enough, wealthy enough, or even after a church had built their own building. Mission emerges as a part of the life of the church from the very beginning. Newbigin maintained that spiritual health depends on the broader vision of world evangelization. Churches that reflect these concepts are missional churches. They understand that mission is the nature of the church from the beginning.

When I was a missionary in Argentina, Bruno Radi, former regional director for the mission work of the Church of the Nazarene in South America, talked about the difference between our calling/vocation and our employment. "My calling," Bruno explained, "is to be a Christian witness to my neighbors. My employment is to be regional director." That perception of calling, or vocation, proves crucial for us. Missionaries are not missionaries because they have a salary or a contract, any more than a church is missional because it has a missions program. We all are missional as we embrace our true vocation to be Christian.

SO WHAT?

So what does all this mean for us? As a beginning, let me suggest seven emphases.

Christian

It means, first and foremost, that we are called to *be* Christian. Before any emphasis on goals, programs, and activities, we are called to draw into God's holy presence. If God's nature is mission, then those of us who partake in his nature will share that same nature of mission. In this sense, therefore, mission is not a program, but rather the essence of being Christian.

Missionary/Missional

It means that the whole church is the missionary. We all are sent. This means we intentionally focus our activities during the week in such a way that we are in contact with people who are not Christians. As missional Christians, we make it a point to learn their culture and to be Christian witnesses as we go.

Sent

It also means that as the church is sent, the whole church also sends missionaries. In a missional church, all members are actively involved in prayer, giving, and learning, while some members are sent to be short-term volunteer missionaries or specialized, long-term missionaries.

Not Only from the West

It means that mission does not flow only from the West. Communities of believers in any part of the globe, transformed by the gospel, engage in God's mission. This implies models of interdependence, in which we see the whole church involved in the whole mission to the whole world. This interdependence does not mean the church in the West has lost its call to missions. It means, rather, that we must share resources with Christians in other parts of the world who have different types of resources to utilize.

A Different Way of Being Church

In many ways, it means a different way of being church. We have often separated ourselves from other Christian groups with the objective of "keeping the faith" by defending our specific emphasis. Given the perspective that the mission is God's mission and not ours, however, the greatest enemy is not other Christians. Our greatest enemy is that we draw into ourselves and become a sectarian group with an inward focus on ourselves instead of outward to God and his mission.

Enemy : draw into selves

Engaged in Justice and Reconciliation

It means the church joins God's activities of justice and reconciliation in those places where social systems and power structures allow for the destruction of well-being and of human life. We have not developed this implication of a missional church in this chapter, but it is part of a holistic understanding of God's mission in and to the world.

Working for Restoration of Creation

It means we participate in what God is doing to restore God's creation. Too often, we have connected this aspect of God's mission to political or special interest groups. However, if we truly are engaged in God's mission, we cannot ignore the fact that we are called to participate in God's activity to care for and restore all God's creation.

BEYOND TRENDY

For some churches, being missional is a matter of style, with elements such as having a pastor with a goatee and playing indie rock music during a service. For others, being missional is just another program applied to attract more people to come into the church. Being a missional church, however, isn't about being trendy, nor is it about methods that will increase statistics. Being a missional church involves being the body of Christ and joining God in God's mission both locally and globally.

Some churches have signs, visible to parishioners as they leave the parking lot, reading, "You are now entering the mission field." This is a good practice, but it carries great implications that go well beyond mere rhetoric. I recently attended a conference featuring (among others) Oscar Muriu, pastor of the Nairobi Chapel church, Nairobi, Kenya.[3] Discussing some of the challenges within the short-term mission movement, he referred to the well-known Korean group that went to Afghanistan in 2007; they were kidnapped, then released after payment of a ransom. The decision to pay for their release has resulted in incredible difficulty for mission efforts. The problem, stated Muriu, was not that this short-term mission group went to Afghanistan. The problem was that they saw their mission activity *only* as short-term and were not willing to die.

Muriu continued by saying there is a place for affluent North American (and Korean) Christians in missions, but only if they share in the cross of Christ. Some may argue this is an oversimplification of a complex situation. The reality remains, however, that being missional is not a matter of taking overseas short-term mission trips, of having a program of missions, or of changing the style of a worship service. Being missional is being desperate for an authentic relationship with God that results in participating in *God's* passion—*God's* mission-nature—reaching to "the nations" in every activity of our lives.

Missiologist Andrew Kirk has said it well, "The Church is by nature missionary to the extent that, if it ceases to be missionary, it has not just failed in one of its tasks, it has ceased being Church."[4] We live in a time of incredible opportunity, in which the triune God calls the church to be the missionary and to join in God's mission of seeking and saving that which is lost.

PART I
TRACING THE *MISSIO DEI* IN SCRIPTURE

2

THE CREATION AS MISSIONAL PARADIGM

Joseph Coleson

◆

As a child, I used to fall asleep to the rhythm of the revolving beacon of the Lake Michigan lighthouse outside my upstairs bedroom window, once the autumn leaves had fallen and no longer obstructed the view. I've gotten wet (I wouldn't quite call it swimming!) in the five Great Lakes, the North Pacific, the South Pacific, the North Atlantic, the Persian Gulf, and Israel's four seas: the Med, the Dead, the Red, and Galilee. I've taken the ferry to the Orkneys from John O'Groats ("The Last House in Scotland"), where the waters of the North Atlantic and the North Sea collide.

I've watched the mist rise from the glassy Charles on perfect fall mornings in Boston, the premier center of American higher education. I've seen seven peaks of the Cascades from the summit of Mount Hood, and looked into Mount St. Helens' crater, where the next step would have been two thousand feet and vertical. I've hiked alone through the countryside of southern England where Thomas Hardy set most of his novels. I've wakened at midnight from a chilled sleep and hiked several hours to meet the sunrise on the summit of Mount Sinai. In Egypt I've hiked through the Valley of the Kings, the Valley of the Queens, and Hatshepsut's funerary temple in a single day. I've hiked from Jerusalem through the Judean wilderness to sleep at the edge of the Dead Sea. I've seen the conies of Proverbs 30:26 sunning themselves on the rocks near the Sea of Galilee. In the strength of the gasoline engine I've traveled the length of the Holy Land twice in thirty-six hours. From the crest of the Great Dividing Range, I've looked into Australia's outback west of Toowoomba, and have snorkeled the Great Barrier Reef off Carnes. I've crossed the Russian steppes that defeated Napoleon and Hitler.

Now, this is not about me, in case you're wondering, except to thank God for blessing me abundantly in the wonders of creation God has privileged me to see and experience. Many reading these words have been to more, and perhaps more exotic, places. If you are one of them, I hope you have also experienced it all as great blessing.

WHY DID GOD CREATE?

Around the globe, we have only to slow down and engage our senses to experience places and scenes that are soul-stirringly beautiful. But do you ever wonder what God is *really* up to? Given the evidence of God's joy in creation, evidence prominent both in Scripture and in nature itself, we may infer that God's motivation to create included sheer joy. But it can't be *only* the joy of creation; if creation were *everything,* we would have to wonder why God included angels and humans who could rebel?

The universe cannot be *only* an exercise in sovereignty, either, though Christians (and many others) believe God ultimately is sovereign. If sovereignty were *everything,* God would be even *less* likely to have opened the door to the troubles brought on by a certain angel-turned-devil and, following him, by the human race. We could pose other possibilities, but each would meet with the same objection: why include potential rebels, if this were the central reason for making a universe, and a world of sensate and spiritual creatures?

I believe both the Bible and the natural order teach that God's original and ultimate mission, at least with respect to humans, was/is to form an "other"—a class of creatures capable of relationship with God, with each other, and with the rest of God's creation. Incredible as it seems, God's mission included even making this relationship eternal through the Incarnation, as Jesus Christ, second person of the Trinity, became human in the womb of his virgin mother.

FINITE, THEREFORE *PHYSICAL*

How does the creation itself reflect this? One part of the answer is that relationship is possible only with communication. Moreover, finite, created beings, at least, cannot communicate unmediated. We need a medium or set of media, a mechanism or set of mechanisms, by which to communicate with our Creator and with each other. Whether God *could* have created something other than the physical universe God *did* create is a moot point. God chose to supply the mechanisms for the various relationships of finite created beings by creating the spiritual-physical universe we inhabit, this universe of space and time, of matter and energy. Even the contemplative spiritual life, though it may draw apart from other persons, does not draw apart from nature. Not only because it cannot, but because it recognizes in nature an aid, a teacher. We are spiritual creatures, but we also are embodied creatures. Food, drink, work, play, rest—all these and more are bodily functions, but each also is a spiritual function, or it is when we function as God designed us to function. We find spiritual joy as well as physical pleasure in being and in doing, and we give both joy and pleasure mutually and reciprocally, when we conduct our relationships with integrity.

We glimpse this in the recently opened vistas of knowledge of the workings of the brain: cognition, recognition, memory, evaluation and decision, and all the rest. The subcellular components of our makeup, and the intricate systems by which they work, are so miniaturized and complex in their workings that scientists in the field tell us it is difficult at the frontiers of this new knowledge and limited understanding to say what is brain, what is mind, what is spirit, what is soul—in short, new discoveries appear to be confirming the holistic biblical understanding of the human person created in the image of God.

FINITE, PHYSICAL, AND *GOOD*

The first and most comprehensive biblical passage on God's creation is Genesis 1. Six times, this chapter reports, God evaluated what God just had made. The conclusion for each and every part of the creation? "God saw that it was *good*" (Gen. 1:4, 10, 12, 18, 21, 25, emphasis added).* The seventh evaluation, following upon God's creation of the first human pair, is comprehensive and vastly more emphatic: "Then God saw *all* that [God] had made and, behold, it was *very* good" (v. 31, emphasis added).

---

*All Scripture quotations in this chapter are the translation of the chapter author, except where noted.

In its theology, in its literary structure and flow, in all its aspects, it is impossible to overstate the importance of this assessment—*God's* assessment—of every part of the unspoiled creation as *very good.* Everything *existed* as God intended, and everything *functioned* as God intended.

Of course, the human rebellion recounted in Genesis 3 damaged God's *very good* creation. However, even in its present state of "futility . . . bondage to decay . . . [and] groaning and travailing together" (Rom. 8:19-22), the natural order witnesses to its Creator. The psalmist asserted that "the heavens declare the glory of God" (Ps. 19:1, NIV; cf. also Pss. 8; 104). God's rhetorical questions of Job (chaps. 38—39) reveal a world of natural intricacy and beauty bound to arouse wonder in all but the most jaded observer.

Ecclesiastes 1:5-7 summarizes the hydrological cycle; this astute ancient observer knew the self-regulation of natural systems, if not the scientific detail of their mechanisms. The exuberant joy of the lovers celebrated in the Song of Songs is not centered only in each other, though human love definitely is an important aspect of God's good creation. The young man and the maiden took pleasure and joy also in the beauty, the wonder, and the intimacy of their outdoor trysting-places. This explicit reveling in our human physicality was and is sanctioned by God, when enjoyed appropriately, as these young lovers took care to do.

One could debate whether Hosea's luxuriant vision is intended as historical or apocalyptic. Whichever, its invitation resonates to the deepest levels of human longing, "Then I will make for them a covenant on that day with the [wild] creatures of the field, and with the birds of the air and the creeping things of the ground. . . . On that day I will respond, says the Lord, I will respond to the heavens and they shall respond to the earth; and the earth shall respond to the grain, the wine, and the oil, and they shall respond to Jezreel; and I will sow him for myself in the land" (Hos. 2:18a, 21-23a). So, too, does Amos's promise gladden the heart of the hearer: one day the plowman shall overtake the reaper, and the treader of grapes the one who sows the seed—earth's abundance running the agricultural cycle into itself on both ends of the year (Amos 9:13).

Throughout his earthly ministry, Jesus maintained intimate contact with nature. He regularly slipped away alone in the early morning darkness to pray (e.g., Mark 1:35); on a mountain retreat, he selected the Twelve (Mark 3:13-19); hearing of his cousin John's murder-by-proxy, he withdrew into a "wilderness place by himself" (Matt. 14:13); his Transfiguration occurred on a mountain height (Luke 9:28 ff.). Even on the night before his death, Jesus withdrew into a garden that, John noted, he often had used as a meeting place (John 18:1-2). To list Jesus' many teachings from nature in his discourses and his parables would be to belabor the obvious, but we may mention the familiar parable of the sower (Matt. 13:3-9), or his assessment of Solomon-in-all-his-glory as poorly dressed by comparison with the wild, untended lilies (Luke 12:27-28). Both in his daily life and in his teaching, Jesus experienced nature as good, instructive, restorative, and even comforting.

We need not wonder at this. After all, Paul reminds us, "All things through him and for him have been created and . . . in him hold together" (Col. 1:16-17).

How, then, is creation missional? It is (among other purposes) the setting in and through which God's people learn to deduce God's character manifested in the continuing goodness of creation, and the magnitude of our privilege of mirroring God's character, because we are created in God's image. Of course, this does not eliminate the need for the special revelation of Scripture or the work of the Holy Spirit. Rather, the creation, as a kind of junior tutor, supplements both.

This leaves not even the pinprick of an opening for gnosticism, that set of doctrines opining that spirit is good and matter, evil—what a pure soul must strive to escape. Gnosticism in all its forms, whether ancient and pagan or modern and disguised as "Christian," is an insult to God, an insidious false piety. God's creation is good; it is joyous. *God* takes joy in God's good creation, from the vastness of uncounted galaxies to the miniature universe of the atom. God's joy is apparent in the *bodily* life of every creature great and small, *each* one—of the trillions that have lived—a unique individual within its species, yet each framed with the same basic building block, the staggeringly complex biological cell. To damn the good creation, even as it awaits restoration, is to accuse God of perjury.

FINITE, PHYSICAL, GOOD, AND *RELATIONAL*

How is creation missional?

As we've noted, one important purpose of God's creation is to facilitate communication with God, with our fellow finite creatures and, because it is the medium and it is here, with the physical world itself. Everything noted above already demonstrates this, directly or indirectly. We may add Isaiah's prediction, "The mountains and the heights will break forth in your presence with joyous shouts, and all the trees of the open country will clap their hands" (Isa. 55:12). The affirmation of Psalm 19:1 is well-known, "The heavens are declaring the glory of God." But Psalm 98 goes further. After extolling God's salvation wonders in all the earth (vv. 1-3), and urging humans to joyful response by all available means (vv. 4-6), the psalmist exhorted the natural world to join the symphony of praise, "Let the sea thunder [its praise], and all its fullness; the earth, and those [humans and others] who dwell in it. Let the streams clap their hands, and let the mountains joyfully sing as one before Yahweh, for he comes to judge the earth. He will judge the world with righteousness, and the peoples with uprightness" (vv. 7-9). All nature benefits from Yahweh's salvation and righteous governance; all nature is called to partner with us in joyous, exuberant celebration and praise.

Another relational purpose for God's physical creation is to give humans (at least) a foundational sense of being and worth. We exist in this world, and interact with it, as well as with each other. Each of us has a name, and in our various communities we bear names and descriptors together. Each of us exists in a place, and many of these descriptors we bear because of the various places we occupy. In the modern world, many of us move from place to place and make our own marks in each new place we enter. We do significant and fulfilling work, possible only by God's creation of all that is, and our varied relationships with all of it, human and nonhuman. It is partly in, through, and with creation that we learn and practice integrity in all our relationships.

FINITE, PHYSICAL, GOOD, RELATIONAL, AND *REDEMPTIVE*

How is creation missional?

In the innocent world of Eden, the human pair turned their backs on God. The intimate companionship they had known with God, with each other, and with their fellow creatures vanished. So accomplished a Creator is God, however, that even the damaged, diminished world after Eden can help us learn repentance and humility, and can demonstrate the importance of empathy with our fellow humans and with the rest of creation.

With all its hardships, griefs, and even its current subjection to un-relenting death (partly because of these, rather than in spite of them), in this nicked-up world we still can learn perseverance and the maturity of delayed gratification. Amid the disappointments of broken relationships, we still can learn joy, because many important relationships do *not* break; they grow. Because Jesus lived and died, as we do, *within* the best and the worst of this good-but-disordered creation, we can learn from him faithfulness unto death. Because Christ loved us unto death *within* creation, we can learn love.

This is but a beginning and we are constrained to move on, for now. Let me encourage you to ponder daily God's already-but-not-yet redemptive work, both in your own life and in your corner of God's good creation.

FINITE, PHYSICAL, GOOD, RELATIONAL, REDEMPTIVE, AND *ESCHATOLOGICAL*

How is creation missional?

Because on the temporal morning of the third day God freed Jesus from the physical prison of a rock-cut tomb, we can learn hope. Isaiah foretold this event as a lavish banquet for "all the peoples" in which the most important course would be God's own; God would "swallow death for all time" (Isa. 25:8). Paul's picture also came from everyday life in the material world, the most common and critical of ancient agricultural practices. A grain of wheat falls into the earth and dies, but in its death is its resurrection life. Just so, in his release from the previously unconquer-able prison of death, Jesus' resurrection, Paul teaches, is the basis for a hardheaded, realistic hope for our own and the rest of creation's deliver-ance from sin, diminishment, and death. In his self-emptying, the *kenōsis* of Paul's sublime christological hymn (Phil. 2:7), Jesus gifted all creation, not just humans, with its original, God-intended fulfillment.

We can be confident the creation is involved and incorporated in God's mission, because the creation is included in the *eschaton*. In biblical terms, we define the *eschaton* not just as the consummation, the grand but narrow point of transition from time to eternity, but as the *telos*, the end toward which God is moving everything to full redemption and restoration. The *telos* is a new heaven and a new earth—not *no* heaven and *no* earth (Isa. 65:17; 66:22; Rev. 21:1).

Isaiah saw this already in his eschatological visions, though he probably did not understand all he saw (and neither do we). He spoke of the Highway of Holiness, by which "the ransomed of Yahweh shall return and come with exultant singing to Zion, and everlasting joy shall be upon their heads; they shall find gladness and joy, but sorrow and sighing shall flee" (35:10). We have noted already God's banquet "for all the peoples" when God will swallow death "for all time" (25:6, 8). One more will have to suffice; Isaiah foresaw a day when "the wolf and the lamb shall graze as one . . . they shall do no evil nor shall they destroy in all my holy mountain, says Yahweh" (65:25).

Once we begin to notice, the announcements multiply, and we realize God's eschatological agenda of redemption and restoration is not reserved for the "end times." This is what God has been about all along, as the pronouncement from the throne affirms, "Behold, I am making all things new" (Rev. 21:5*a*).

CONCLUSION

We have but begun. God's restoration of God's good creation is integral to the gospel, the good news, partly because we are integral to the creation. Our existence as physical creatures teaches us how to encounter, interact, love, play, work—in short, to be the spiritual-physical beings God created us to be. The present earth is our nursery, playground, laboratory, apprenticeship, and schoolroom for what lies beyond. What that is, we cannot now begin to imagine, Paul tells us (1 Cor. 2:9), but it will not be completely other than the here and now. It will be a continuation, the continuation of the stalk of golden grain from the single seed fallen into the ground. It will be the continuation between the lips of a mother on her infant's cheek, and the lips of lovers on their wedding night. In their places, both are valid, valuable, delightful, holy. But the wedding night requires two mature persons, and maturity requires time, practice, experience, learning. Humans learn maturity by living in God's good creation.

3

THE MISSION OF GOD AND A COVENANT PEOPLE

Roger L. Hahn

═══════════════ ◆ ═══════════════

The mission of God may be described as God's intention and activity to restore all creation to the purposes for which he created it. The overarching story of the whole of Scripture provides clear evidence of God's mission. The opening chapters of Genesis and a variety of other biblical texts portray the order, beauty, and purposes of creation. Genesis 3—6 and many other biblical texts show how human disobedience leads to the devastating loss of the order, beauty, and purposes of creation.

One of the first evidences of God's mission of restoring creation appears in Genesis 6—9. By the flood God destroyed the evil so prevalent throughout the earth and preserved righteous and blameless Noah, along with his family. However, Genesis 9—11 makes quite clear that creation was not restored to its original glory. Sin's consequences were becoming increasingly harmful to the creation in general and humanity in particular. When Scripture is viewed as a whole, God's mission begins with the call to Abram in Genesis 12. It continues through the Bible to its successful (and future) climax by the end of Revelation.

In recent centuries the Christian culture of the West has focused more and more on individualism and one's private relationship with God. As a result an important aspect of God's mission is often forgotten. God's mission is ultimately corporate. God desires more than the salvation of a certain number of individual persons. God wants a people who model already the restoration that is still underway in the world. God began with a person in order to gain a nation. He then worked with that nation to gain the whole world. The word "covenant" describes God's act of entering into relationship with that person, that nation, and the world. Biblical scholar Walter Brueggemann describes covenant as "perhaps the central and defining theological affirmation of the Old Testament."[1]

Genesis 6:18 and 9:9-17 speak of a covenant between God and Noah. However, most Bible scholars identify four primary covenants within Scripture: the Abrahamic, the Mosaic, the Davidic, and the new covenants. The basic concept of covenant in the ancient Near East was that of a bond binding people together in a relationship of allegiance to a king. The concept is somewhat like the modern idea of a treaty. A covenant could be entered into voluntarily by equals or could be imposed on another by a superior power. The words most often associated with covenant in ancient civilizations come in two pairs. The first pair is oath and commitment, demonstrating the faithful bond established by the covenant. The second is love and friendship, expressing the ideal benefits of the covenant. The covenants of the Bible are always imposed by God (or Christ). However, they demonstrate the graciousness of God, rather than fickleness. Whether in the foreground or the background the themes of mutual commitment and love are always present in the major biblical covenants.

THE ABRAHAMIC COVENANT

God initiated a covenant with Abram in Genesis 12:1-3, though the word "covenant" does not appear in these verses. Apparently out of the blue, God called Abram and issued him two commands. The first (Gen. 12:1) was to go from his country, from his family, and from his father's house to the land that God would show him. Verse 2 identifies three consequences of obedience to this command. First, God would make Abram a great nation. Second, God would bless Abram. Third, God would make Abram's name great. Though English versions rarely translate the Hebrew imperative as a command, the second command appears at the end of verse 2. There Abram is commanded to be a blessing. Verse 3 gives three consequences of obedience. First, God would bless those who blessed Abram (and his nation). Second, God would curse those who cursed Abram. Third, in (or by) Abram all the families of the earth would be blessed (or will bless themselves).

The multiple references to blessing in verses 2-3 echo the blessings God pronounced upon the good creation in Genesis 1:22, 28; and 2:3. This emphasis on blessing signaled God's intention to restore the nations of the earth to the good order of creation through Abram. It is clear from this promise that not just Abram (or the nation that would come from him) but all the families of the earth would be blessed. Thus those families would also be restored to God's creation purposes.

Genesis 15:18 and several verses in Genesis 17 specifically mention the covenant between God and Abram. These texts narrow the focus but expand the details of the call to Abram found in Genesis 12. In Genesis 15 Abram questioned how his having no child fit with the promise that God would make him a great nation. God assured Abram that he would produce offspring and that they eventually would be as hard to count as the stars of the heavens. God also revealed that the path to such blessing would not be smooth. Abram's offspring would be enslaved in a foreign land for four hundred years. Then God would bring them back and continue the plan of restoration. Genesis 15 also promises land to Abram's descendants. That land would stretch from Canaan's border with Egypt in the southwest to the Euphrates River in the north.

Genesis 17 repeats the covenantal promise to Abram to possess the land of Canaan and to become the ancestor of many nations. God also changed Abram's name to Abraham (v. 5) as perpetual evidence of the promise that he would be the father of many nations. God called this covenant with Abraham an everlasting covenant. God also established the circumcision of every male descendant of Abraham as a physical sign of the covenant. These covenant details described in Genesis 15 and 17 made clearer how God intended to make Abraham a great nation. With the fulfillment of that promise beginning, Scripture can turn its attention to the way that nation would become a blessing to all the earth.

THE MOSAIC COVENANT

The narrative of Genesis 12 through Exodus 24 describes how Abraham became a great nation. Abraham's offspring went into Egypt and became a nation that suffered but survived years of slavery. Finally, that nation came out of slavery in Egypt and began its journey home to Canaan as a mighty and populous nation. Exodus 19—24 describes the establishment and basic content of the Mosaic covenant. (It is often called the Sinai covenant because God entered into this covenant with Israel at Mount Sinai.) Exodus 19 and 24 describe the covenant-making ceremony between God and Israel. Chapters 20—23 record the content of the covenant. They often are called The Book of the Covenant by Bible scholars.

Though God "imposed" this covenant on Israel, it was a covenant of grace. This is clear from God's first words to Israel in Exodus 19:4. He stated, "You saw what I did to the Egyptians and I lifted you up on eagles' wings and I brought you to myself."* The opening line of the covenant content makes the same point. Exodus 20:2 reads, "I am the LORD your God who brought you up out of the land of Egypt, out of the house of slavery." Before God asked anything of Israel he rescued that nation from slavery in Egypt. Thus, in the Mosaic covenant the saving grace of God comes before God's commands that Israel participate in the covenant and in God's mission. God carried out his mission of restoration for Israel before asking Israel to join in that mission of restoring others.

The missional character of the Mosaic covenant is most clearly stated in Exodus 19:5-6. "Now if you will truly obey my voice and keep my covenant, then you will be my treasured possession from all peoples, for all the earth is mine. You will be a kingdom of priests for me and a holy nation." Verse 5 speaks of the Mosaic covenant for the first time in Scripture. It affirms God's election of Israel to special status and the responsibility of obedient covenant keeping. Verse 5 also sets the context of Israel's selection in terms of the whole earth. This raises the important question of Israel's status and purpose. What is the relationship between God's choosing Israel as his treasured possession and God's statement that he had chosen Israel from all the peoples? Terrence Fretheim comments, "The best sense may be captured in this translation: *Because* all the earth is mine, so you, you shall be to me a kingdom of priests and a holy nation. This suggests that the phrases relate to a mission that encompasses God's purposes for the entire world. *Israel is commissioned to be God's people on behalf of the earth which is God's.*"[2] The key missional elements appear in verse 6. Israel is to be a kingdom of priests and a holy nation.

The concept of a kingdom of priests would have been immediately clear to Israel, but it is hard for modern Christians to understand. In Israel's practice and cultural world, a priest, as worship and civil leader, had

---

*All Scripture quotations in this chapter are the translation of the chapter author.

a representative role. The high priest was not just the most honored priest with the most special privileges. The high priest was the representative for the whole priestly family (the family of Aaron in the Mosaic period). He represented his family to God and he represented God to his priestly family. The priestly family was not just the most honored family of Israel. They represented God to the tribe of Levi and represented the tribe of Levi to God. The tribe of Levi was not just the most special tribe of Israel. The Levites had the responsibility of representing God to all Israel and all Israel to God.

Likewise being a kingdom (or nation) of priests did not mean Israel could understand herself simply as God's favorite people. Rather, Israel was to be a priestly nation representing God to all the world and representing all the world to God. Thus the phrase "kingdom of priests" clearly envisions Israel participating in the mission of God for the restoration of all peoples. To accomplish this purpose Israel had to be a "holy nation." Authentic participation in God's mission required that Israel become "sharers in the divine nature" (2 Pet. 1:4). Becoming sharers of God's holiness gives one indication of the restoration of all creation to which God's mission is committed.

Exodus 19 and 24 give evidence of the relationship between God's holiness and the covenant. God's holiness has to do with God being "Wholly Other" and distinct from Israel. This is clear by the boundaries set for Israel, keeping them at the foot of Mount Sinai and forbidding them to touch the mountain. Exodus 19:10, 14, 22 speak of the need for Israel to be holy because of being in covenant relationship with God. Exodus 20—23 expresses God's expectations for Israel being distinct or set apart through a series of commandments. These commandments were to shape Israel's behavior in every area of life. The first commandments, commonly known as the Ten Commandments, provide an overview of the holy life to which God summons his people. This holy life was necessary so that Israel might participate in God's mission.

The Mosaic covenant set in place a comprehensive way of life by which Israel would be the restored and missional people of God in the world. The covenant defined the nature of relationship between God and Israel. The relationship was often summarized by the expression, "I will be their [Israel's] God and they will be my people." That relationship could not be authentic if the covenant were only "imposed" by God. Both in Exodus 19:8 and 24:3 Israel responded, "All [the words] which the LORD has spoken we will do." Thus the covenant relationship is characterized by mutuality. God saves, God promises, and God commands. Israel promises, Israel obeys, and Israel becomes sharers of God's holiness and God's mission. As a relationship, the covenant is both entered into once and for all time and must be renewed periodically.

Covenant renewal, in which Israel recommitted itself to this relationship with God, plays an important role in the Old Testament. In Deuteronomy 5:2-3, Moses states that the covenant of Mount Sinai was made with all the Israelites standing before him ready to enter Canaan. In fact, the covenant had been made with the parents of those Israelites. The point of Deuteronomy 5:2-3 is that the covenant is a living relationship that must become a reality in each new generation. According to Deuteronomy 29:14-15 the covenant is made not just for the generation that would enter Canaan. It is also made with future generations "who are not here with us today." Further accounts of covenant renewal can be found in Joshua 8:30-35; 24:1-28; 2 Kings 11:17-18; 23:1-3; Ezra 10:1-5; and Nehemiah 8—10. Despite these periodic renewals of the Sinai covenant, Israel's disobedience thwarted the accomplishment of God's mission. The restoration God desired for both Israel and the world did not take place.

THE DAVIDIC COVENANT

The Mosaic covenant with Israel became the vehicle by which the Abrahamic covenant might be fulfilled. In a similar way the Davidic covenant became a means to accomplish the missional purpose of the Sinai covenant. The word "covenant" is not used in 2 Samuel 7:11-29, where God promised the relationship now called the Davidic covenant. However, 2 Samuel 23:5 and Psalm 89:3, 28 call the promises made to David in 2 Samuel 7:11-29 God's covenant with David. Like the Abrahamic covenant, the covenant with David was made with an individual but included promises to his descendants.

God's promise to David in 2 Samuel 7:11-13 is that God would make David a "house." The following verses make it clear that the "house" is not a building in which to live, but a family of descendants. Further, God would establish the family of David's descendants on David's throne. Though political concerns permeate the Davidic covenant, David's response to God in 2 Samuel 7:18-29 echoes the covenant summary. This is clear in the words, "You established for yourself your people Israel to be your people forever and you, Lord, became their God." David understood the covenant God was making with him as a way to fulfill the national covenant of Sinai.

The missional character of the Davidic covenant also appears in David's response to God at the end of 2 Samuel 7:19. The wide variety of translations of a phrase there indicates considerable confusion about David's meaning. Some translations construct the phrase as a question, some as a statement, and some as an exclamation of hope. In the Hebrew text, David describes God's promise of a perpetual kingdom for his descendants as *torah ha-adam*. The word *torah* is often translated "Law." However, its basic meaning in Hebrew is instruction and especially instruction for the ordering of life. Most English-speaking Christians only know *adam* as a proper name for the first human. Hebrew authors used it throughout the Old Testament to refer to humanity or humankind. Thus David received the promise that God would establish his descendants on his throne forever as a promise for instruction of all humankind.

It was not immediately clear how the Davidic covenant would become instruction for the ordering of all humanity's life. For several hundred years the promise was taken as divine authority for the continuing Davidic dynasty. But the destruction of the temple and the Babylonian Exile called into question the promise of the Davidic covenant. God's promise appeared to be broken. God appeared to have forsaken the Davidic covenant, as generations passed without a king in Jerusalem. The political heritage of the Davidic dynasty reappeared among the Jews in their hope for a Messiah. This Messiah would be a descendant of David, restore Israel to political prominence, and sit once again on the throne of David. But the missional heritage of the Davidic covenant took a different turn.

THE NEW COVENANT

Jeremiah received the sad assignment of declaring the destruction of Jerusalem and the temple. He stated often that failure to obey the Sinai covenant was the reason for the coming destruction. He alone of all the Old Testament authors used the words "new covenant" to refer to God's restoration of his people. This passage, Jeremiah 31:31-34, has several echoes in the New Testament and is quoted in full in Hebrews 8:8-12. However, similar themes appear in Ezekiel 34—37 and in various texts in Isaiah 42, 49, 54, and 55.

Jeremiah stated that the new covenant would not be like the Sinai covenant that God's people broke. However, the difference was not a matter of content but of a more intimate relationship between God and his people. The new covenant would be God's law written on the hearts of God's people (Jer. 31:33). The Sinai covenant finally would become reality. God would be their God, and they would become God's people. It no longer would be necessary for God's people to urge each other to know God because the relationship with God envisioned in the Mosaic covenant would be fulfilled. As Jeremiah 31:34 states, "for they will all know me, from the least of them to the greatest."

As Christians well know, the dual themes of the new covenant and the Messiah come together in the person of Jesus Christ. By his atoning life, death, and resurrection, the church came into being as the new covenant community. God calls the church to participate in God's mission of restoring all creation to God's creation purposes. The instruction (*torah*) for all humankind is written on the hearts of believers. This is the work of the Holy Spirit empowering the church to join in the mission of God.

CONCLUSION

The New Testament's adoption of covenant/new covenant language means we should understand the church as a covenant people. That means that the church owes obedience to God. But more importantly it signals that God calls the church to participate in God's missional purpose of restoring all creation. The missional work of the church is not the calling of a few isolated individuals who serve alone on the front lines of ministry. Participation in the mission of God does not ask whether it is carried out in one's own culture or cross-culturally. The missional work of the church is a corporate calling for the church to be the people who represent God to the world and who bring the world to God.

4

LET JUSTICE ROLL DOWN
THE MISSION OF GOD IN COMMUNITY
Joseph Coleson

Most of us recall the story of Ruth, the young Moabite, and her Israelite mother-in-law, Naomi. Both were widows when Naomi returned from Moab to Bethlehem about 1100 B.C., with Ruth at her side. Arriving as the barley harvest began, they faced a large problem. To provide food, Ruth went out to glean. By the end of the story, Ruth and Boaz were married and Naomi was a grandmother through Boaz's legal arrangements. Boaz and Ruth became great-grandparents of David and part of the lineage of Jesus, David's greater Son, Israel's Messiah, and the world's Savior. Ruth's story attracts us because it vividly illustrates, in the microcosm of ancient Israelite village life, God's missional intention of community, expressed with generous integrity and superabundant grace.

Fast forward with me nearly four hundred years. The prophet Micah hailed from Moresheth, a rural town in the Judean lowlands, only about twenty miles southwest of Bethlehem. Micah's short book indicts Judah's rich and powerful, who had found many ways to pervert God's mission to their own material gain. In Micah 2:9, we find the pathos of the betrayal of God's missional care for every Judean family in poignant words striking the hearer as both passionate accusation and sorrowful lament: "The women of my people you drive away, each from her delightful house. From her children, you take my splendor forever."* The most vulnerable of God's people were thrown aside without remorse, for the convenience and further enrichment of the powerful few.

---

*All Scripture quotations in this chapter are the translation of the chapter author, except where noted.

It would be difficult to exaggerate the contrasts between these two scenes. In Ruth and Boaz's Bethlehem, we see a near-idyllic fulfillment, for its time, of God's missional purposes for ancient Israel. Community, genuine witness outside the community, genuine welcome into the community, love, justice, mercy, grace, eschatological hope—all these and more are here. They permeate this story, a sublime example of God's mission, intended ultimately to reach all persons and all peoples. Four centuries later, Micah's lament easily could have been set in Bethlehem, Moresheth, or a hundred other small Judean towns, all of them oppressed by the wealthy and powerful centered in Jerusalem. Kings, nobles, priests, international merchants—all had conspired in the City of Peace to legalize the corruption of God's mission of peace and well-being (*shalom*) intended for *all* God's people, all the while flaunting their hypocritical piety in the temple.

God's Passion for God's Mission

It would be difficult, also, to overestimate the value *God* has placed on God's creation vision of human well-being in community. This is *why* God created us in the first place: for relationships of integrity and appropriate intimacy with God, with each other, and with the rest of creation. God began, of course, in Eden, with a garden planted to nurture and teach our first parents in that first and perfect community (see chapter 1). Soon, however, they chose a fatal "independence." If the biblical record of God's mission means anything, we can know that God, though not surprised, was deeply grieved. Yet God did not give up on the mission, but moved to redeem humanity and, with us, all the earthly creation. This is God's passionate intention, and God will not be deterred.

God set in motion the missional program of rescue and redemption with Abraham and Sarah (Gen. 12). Generations later, God invited Israel into a new missional partnership through the Mosaic covenant offered and accepted at Sinai (see chapter 3). Joshua led Israel into Canaan and oversaw the allotment of land to Israel's tribes. God planned their settlement as a new thing in the post-Eden world, modeling God's missional purposes—ultimately, for any and all who would accept God's gracious offer of relationship. In the period of the Judges, Israel wavered between faithlessness and repentance. From this time, and as a beacon of hope in a landscape of distress and despair, we have the book of Ruth, evidence that even then God's missional purposes in and through early Israel could be realized.

GOD'S PROVISION FOR EARLY ISRAEL

One way to understand Israel's life in the land as the early model of God's missional redemptive purpose is to gauge the cosmic distance between Israel's social structures and everything else in their world at the time God brought them into Canaan. Egyptians thought their pharaohs were the sun god, Amun-Re, sitting on the throne as Thutmose, Ramses, and so on. These pharaohs had made Canaan part of their empire, but Egyptian power had waned; the small Canaanite city-states now were left mostly to their own devices. Each city, or sometimes a cluster of cities, was ruled by a privileged class: the king and a small group of royal, noble, and other wealthy families, including priests and priestesses of the gods who sanctioned these arrangements. A privileged few were in; most were out and served, directly or indirectly, the palace or the temple. What could the simple folk do? It was the will of the gods.

Against this backdrop of the privileged abusing the poor, God's battles for Israel stand out as history's first war of liberation—the Divine Warrior liberating God's people! Having delivered them from Egyptian bondage, God brought them into Canaan. The Mosaic covenant granted place, livelihood, and standing in the community to all. Anthropologists and historians call early Israel an "agrarian subsistence" society. Nearly every family owned and worked its own small farm, providing nearly everything they needed from their fields, orchards, vineyards, garden, herd, and flock. What little they could not grow or make for themselves, they could trade for, with surplus crops or livestock. Barley and wheat, the cereal grains Ruth gleaned, provided daily bread, making them the most important contribution to every town's food supply.

The only significant "political" needs were justice in cases of crime or civil disputes, and public recognition and recording of the civil transactions provided for in the laws of the covenant. Boaz's purchase of Naomi's field recorded in Ruth 4, rich with legal and cultural information, is an example from this time of God's missional concern for justice and the *shalom* of everyday folk. The council of elders in each town knew the parties involved; the covenant instructed them to judge justly, with unwavering integrity (e.g., Lev. 19:15). In early Israel, cases not resolved at the town level were brought to the leader recognized as God's judge at that time; Deborah is a prominent example (Judg. 4:4-5).

Let us be clear about the innovative nature of God's mission for early Israel. In Canaan (and elsewhere) every person was regarded theologically as temple property, and/or politically as royal property, because priests, priestesses, and kings all were agents of the gods. Ancient Near Eastern documents of many kinds reflect this, referring to the king as "*the man of X country*"; often, subjects were "the king's men," or "the king's servants/slaves." In Israel, the one true God was Owner, but by right of creation. Moreover, God's desire for Israel was not servitude, but freely chosen, intimate, healthy relationships—with God who created *all* humans *for* relationship, with each other, and with the rest of God's good creation. In the Prophets, both the former and the latter, this is expressed as the idyllic picture of "each one [dwelling] in safety under his own vine and under his own fig tree" (e.g., 1 Kings 4:25 [Heb., 5:5]; Mic. 4:4).

THE TEMPTATION TO APPEAR "NORMAL"

God intended this new missional paradigm to attract others. Besides Ruth, the record includes Rahab (Josh. 6:25; Matt. 1:5), the Gibeonites (Josh. 9), and many others. Eventually Israel even absorbed the Canaanites in their midst, but *this* became a major problem. Forgetting God's warnings, Israel allowed Canaan's gods to ensnare them in idolatrous worship. This was not just the option of which worship center to attend. It was the choice between remaining faithful to *God's* mission, on the one hand, and relapsing into the *demonic* mission of enslaving all humans, on the other—the bondage from which God already had freed Israel.

How did the Baals, the gods and goddesses of Canaan and of Israel's other neighbors, become such a compelling attraction for Israel? We may frame an answer in terms of the common human tendency to compare ourselves with our neighbors, rather than keeping our focus on God's invitation to "adventure ourselves with God" (to paraphrase Wesley). Israel began to ask, and we too are prone to ask: Can we really trust God when our structures and institutions look so fragile by comparison with all that our neighbors have? They have a king; we have a judge—sometimes. They have an army, with horses and chariots; we have farmers, and when we capture chariots (May we be so blessed!), God tells us to burn them. They have temples, gods, and goddesses in every city; go inside, and you can see Baal himself, Asherah herself. We have a tent, we can't even get past the outer curtain wall, and God says we're not allowed to honor him anywhere with a gold statue, not even in the inner sanctuary.

Blinded by envy of the wealth of the privileged *few* among their Canaanite neighbors, Israel lost sight of God's daily provision for *every* Israelite, and God's protective blanket of *shalom* upon the community as a whole. Moreover, they failed to notice that Canaan's wealth was blood money, accumulated on the bowed backs of the many poor in every Canaanite city across the land.

Ultimately, Israel demanded of Samuel a king (1 Sam. 8). God usually does not ignore the free will of God's people, though our wrong choices tend to bend and lengthen the path to God's missional goals. Rather, God works with us, though we are weak, timid, wrong, even sinful. So God granted Israel a king—and kings, once established, seldom leave of their own accord. Every free Israelite man now found the king to be "the man"; himself, only "the king's man." Each household now was liable for taxes to support the court, the army, and the bureaucracy. Now, every Israelite's only protection was the king's conscience and, too often, the king did not exhibit a conscience. The parade example is Jezebel, true to her Phoenician roots, convincing her husband Ahab that he, "the man," could seize the property of any Israelite. Naboth lost not only his vineyard, but his life (1 Kings 21).

THE PROPHETS' CALLS TO RETURN TO GOD'S MISSION

Despite Israel's cyclical unfaithfulness, and the wickedness of too many of their kings, God did not abandon either Israel or God's mission, but continued to act missionally. God sent men and women anointed and empowered by the Spirit of God to challenge the wicked and encourage the faithful. In the Hebrew Bible arrangement, the written records of the historians are called the Former Prophets: Joshua, Judges, Samuel, Kings; the written records of the "classical" prophets are called the Latter Prophets: Isaiah, Jeremiah, Ezekiel, the Twelve. In both divisions, Israel's and Judah's kings and elites were judged by: (1) their faithfulness to God; and (2) their justice toward their fellow Israelites, especially toward the poor and the powerless. Most of them, both the historians and the prophets found lacking.

Amos of Tekoa

The classical or "writing" prophets began with Amos and Hosea about 750 B.C. A line from Amos may be the most famous call to justice ever voiced, "But let justice roll down like waters, and righteousness like an ever-flowing stream" (Amos 5:24, NRSV). Amos is well-known also for the *examples* of injustice he highlighted in his short stint as God's missional messenger to the kingdom of Israel. He charged the rich and powerful with selling the righteous for money, that is, to make a profit, rather than observing the law of the kinsman-redeemer and allowing them to work off their debts in the service of a relative. They sold the poor for a debt as small as the price of a pair of sandals (2:6).

When evicting from their ancestral farms those who had fallen into their power because of debt, these greedy creditors even "panted after the dust of the earth on the heads of the poor" (2:7). In other words, they were so greedy for every fraction of a shekel of profit that, for fear of losing a few grains of soil, they made those they evicted comb their fingers through their hair before letting them step off the land that had been God's gift to them. Hyperbole it may be, but it stands as a powerful picture of greed and heartlessness toward those in their clutches. At the same time as they were driving the poor from the land that was their livelihood, the wealthy were building luxurious summer and winter homes for themselves, trimmed and accented with costly imported ivory (3:15). They perverted justice for bribes (5:12). We could list many more, but all illustrate the fact that, living in lavish luxury and pleasure, the wealthy and powerful were callous about the health of God's community, the nation as a whole (6:4-6).

Amos issued his challenge, to let justice roll on like waters, in the central highlands, Israel's homeland, where water is precious, where no stream was (or is today) "ever-flowing," that is, flowing year-round. To compare justice and righteousness with the necessary water of life is to say that no people can live without them, either. Using Assyria as God's rod of judgment, God eliminated all Israel's elite by death or exile, less than thirty years after Amos's visit to Bethel.

Micah of Moresheth

In the south, Micah indicted the rich and powerful of Judah for these same crimes. We have noted already their heartlessness in evicting women and children from their homes (2:9) but, like Amos, Micah also recorded many other specific crimes. One aspect of the prophet's calling was to act as God's "prosecutor"; several used the term "lawsuit" (*rib*, pronounced "reeve") more than once. Micah, however, is remembered also for his clear, compelling *summary* of every person's responsibility (and privilege) spelled out in the various bodies of law, both biblical and beyond. Micah's question is simple, clear, and powerful, "What does Yahweh require of you, but to do justice, and to love lovingkindness, and to walk in humility with your God?" (6:8). This is not negative, but positive. Living in just and generous relationship *with* all promotes *shalom for* all.

Malachi After the Exile

We could multiply our listing of these prophetic calls to justice. The larger point, though, is that when they failed to move Israel and Judah to real and lasting reform, God acted *missionally* even in expelling them from their (from *God's*) land. When justice is perverted too far, ignored too long, it becomes necessary to start over, in a sense—and God knows that timing. The ledger of injustice against the poor, and against the land itself, must be balanced at last. In Judah's case, the seventy years of exile in Babylon gave the land the Sabbath rests it had lost (Jer. 29:10). It did not, however, result in a wholehearted passion for justice in all those privileged to return to Jerusalem and Judah. Malachi called them out for their habit of trading in their wives for younger women (Mal. 2:14-15)— not a modern invention!—and accused them of reverting to practices that had caused Judah's downfall in the first place: oppression of laborers, widows, orphans, and resident aliens (3:5). The prophets could call the nation to account, but even the experience of exile was not enough to turn their hearts toward justice, toward *shalom* in community for all.

WHO WAS, WHO IS, WHO IS TO COME

What, then, *could* do that? Ultimately, the prophets' call for justice is an eschatological vision, but "eschatological" understood in terms of the "already-but-not-yet" kingdom that Jesus proclaimed. God has begun, and calls on God's people as partners, to render perfect justice, to restore victims to their rightful places, and to multiply the people of God.

This last is God's goal too, proclaimed vividly in Isaiah's vision that God would commission God's Servant to bring salvation "to the end of the earth," because it was "too light" a task for him to restore "only" the tribes of Jacob (Isa. 49:6). God never intended Israel to be an only child but, rather, the eldest child, through whom, and through whose witness, God would bring the whole world into the divine family. God's mission is to create the *people* of God; all who accept God's invitation are welcomed. Ultimately, all God's daughters and sons will dwell in safety under God's protection. Even that implacable enemy, death, God will swallow; then God will feast God's people and wipe the tear from every eye (Isa. 25:6-9; Rev. 21:1-7). *That,* finally, is justice and *shalom* in community: the eschaton fully realized, the garden of God in the city of God, home at last with the Lamb of God, the Lion of Judah, our beloved Bridegroom.

CONCLUSION

As it was for ancient Israel, so it is for us. Seeking justice and *shalom* for all is central to Christian life and witness because it still is God's vision and mission. Wesley termed this "acts of mercy," and coupled them with "acts of piety" as the Christian's duty to God and one's fellow creatures. Lest we hear "duty" and think "drudgery," let us remind ourselves that being missional means living daily as the now-and-forever family of God. We have termed God's people "community," but we are more. We are adopted younger siblings ("divine," though not God) of our Elder Brother, Redeemer, and hero. We regard and treat one another as beloved brothers and sisters in Christ. We are privileged to practice, to announce, and to evidence to the ends of the earth God's mission in the here and now. We rejoice and live in the "already," even as we look for the "not yet," the completion of God's mission: eternal *shalom* in God's forever family, purposed before the world was. Let justice roll down? May it be so, Lord, now and forever!

5

THE MISSION OF GOD IN JESUS' TEACHING ON THE KINGDOM OF GOD

Roger L. Hahn

———————————◆———————————

God's mission may be defined as the restoration of all creation to God's creation purposes. Within the grand narrative of Scripture God's sending Christ is the central and climactic expression of God's mission. John 3:17 clearly makes this point, "For God did not send the son into the world in order to condemn the world, but in order that the world might be saved through him."* This basic truth is affirmed in the Synoptic Gospels by the voice from heaven at Jesus' baptism and transfiguration. The fullest expression appears in Matthew 17:5, "This is my beloved Son, in whom I am well pleased. Listen to him."

One certainly would expect that the teachings of Jesus would articulate the mission of God. Without doubt the kingdom of God is the central concept taught by Jesus in the Synoptic Gospels.[1] The gospel of John rarely mentions the kingdom,[2] making life, the life of the eternal God, the central subject of Jesus' teaching, instead. However, in the conversation with Nicodemus in John 3 Jesus brought kingdom language and his teaching on eternal life together. The purpose of this chapter is to identify the most important features of Jesus' teaching about the kingdom of God and to show how that teaching expresses the mission of God.

———————————

*All Scripture quotations in this chapter are the translation of the chapter author.

THE BIBLICAL MEANING OF "KINGDOM"

Jesus probably taught in Aramaic or perhaps in Greek. The linguistic difference between the word "kingdom" in those languages and in modern English is the same. The basic assumption of the Aramaic word *malkuth* and the Greek word *basileia* is dynamic and relational, rather than territorial. These words point toward sovereignty, reign, royal rule, or kingship. The territorial idea of a realm was only a secondary implication, inasmuch as a place would be needed in which to exercise kingly rule. Thus, in the New Testament world there was no kingdom without a king and the kingdom was the king's royal rule. As R. T. France puts it, "'The kingdom of God' is not making a statement about a 'thing' called 'the kingdom,' but about *God,* that he is king."[3]

This is an important distinction for modern persons whose political orientation is to democracies. Their image of a kingdom is primarily the territory ruled by a king, and a king is envisioned as a figurehead with primarily ritual functions. The fact that "kingdom" was relational in biblical times shapes how we understand Jesus' teachings. When Jesus declared in Mark 1:15, "The kingdom of God has come near,"[4] he meant *God* has come near to exercise his divine kingship. The often-used admonition "enter the kingdom" meant to accept the sovereignty of God, to submit to God as king. The essential evidence of a king's sovereignty was a subject's obedience or allegiance. A king's kingship or sovereignty only existed to the degree that he was able to command obedience from subjects. A kingdom was only a place to the degree that it was a place of obedience to the king. This meant that when Jesus spoke of the kingdom of God he was speaking of 100 percent, complete, total obedience to God.

This fundamental understanding of kingdom presented the Jewish world into which Jesus came with both a problem and a hope. The Old Testament had clearly identified God as King (see Ps. 103:19 and Isa. 52:7 as only two examples) and Judaism affirmed God's eternal sovereignty. The problem with this profoundly true affirmation of faith is that the world in general did not obey God. Thus though God's sovereignty was a matter of faith for the Jewish people, it was not an observable reality in the world. Jewish people could not even point to themselves or their own history as examples of total obedience of God. How can God be considered sovereign when people in general and his own people in particular do not obey him? This was a profound problem for the Judaism of Jesus' time (and it is a problem that has not disappeared). So Judaism looked forward in hope to a day when God would be completely obeyed and his sovereignty would be totally acknowledged. They described that day as the kingdom of God. That that day was approaching is what Jesus' listeners understood when they heard him declaring that the kingdom of God had come near.

THE KINGDOM IS ABOUT GOD

The Jewish understanding of the kingdom of God is important for our understanding of Jesus' teaching. However, it only provides a foundational perspective. Jewish teachers developed and applied this basic understanding to the kingdom of God in a variety of ways. For Christians, Jesus' particular interpretation of the kingdom invites us into the mission of God. Foundational for Jesus' teaching of the kingdom is that it was first and foremost about God, rather than about himself. For believers trained to think of the deity of Jesus, it is easy to assume that Jesus' proclamation of God's kingship would be about his own kingship. But careful reading clearly reveals that when Jesus spoke of the kingdom he pointed to the royal rule of God. In theological terms, Jesus' teaching of the kingdom was *theo*centric, rather than *Christo*centric.

THE KING OF THE KINGDOM IS A FATHER

The truth that Jesus was (and is) the Son of God gave rise to the rich picture of God found in Jesus' kingdom teaching. In the words of A. M. Hunter, Jesus taught that "the king in the kingdom is a Father."[5] The fact that Jesus called God *abba* makes it clear that the kingship of God is quite different from the kingship of human tyrants. When the disciples asked him to teach them to pray, Jesus told them to say, "Father, your name must be sanctified, your kingdom must come" (Luke 11:2). After cautioning against seeking food, drink, and clothing, Jesus pointed out, "The Gentiles eagerly seek after all these things, but your Father knows that you have need of them. However, seek his kingdom and these things will be added to you. Do not fear, little flock, because the Father is well-pleased to give you the kingdom" (12:30-32). Perhaps the crowning picture of God as Father comes in the so-called parable of the prodigal son (15:11-32), where the gracious love of God clearly knows no bounds. Jesus' teaching of the kingdom reveals that the mission of God is not judgment, but the passion of a loving Father to restore his wayward children.

THE KINGDOM COMES THROUGH JESUS AND HIS MINISTRY

Jesus understood that the kingdom was centered in God rather than in himself. However, he clearly believed that he played a central role in its coming. People asked him why the disciples of John the Baptist and of the Pharisees fasted, but his disciples did not. Jesus responded, "The guests of the bridegroom cannot fast while the bridegroom is with them" (Mark 2:19). Thus, Jesus certainly believed that he and his ministry were ushering in the celebration of the messianic banquet. This banquet was part of the Jewish expectation of the kingdom. The following verses compare his ministry to new wine that cannot be contained in old wineskins and to a new patch that cannot be sewed onto an old garment. The radical newness of Jesus' ministry was his ministry to lost and broken people. Rather than simply maintaining the religious status quo Jesus participated in God's mission by seeking to restore these people to God's creation purposes. Jesus' claim of authority to forgive sins and his practice of entering into table fellowship with tax collectors and sinners provide important teaching. They are further evidence that he understood that the kingdom was centered in him and his ministry, and that the kingdom was part of God's mission.

THE KINGDOM IS PRESENT IN JESUS' MINISTRY

Jesus believed the kingdom was a present reality. This comes as a surprise to many casual Bible readers. The widespread, but mistaken, idea that the kingdom refers to heaven has often been understood to mean that the kingdom is a future reality. As we will see, Jesus did envision a future consummation of the kingdom, but he clearly taught that the kingdom had become present through his own ministry. Responding to charges that he cast out demons by Beelzebul, Jesus said, "If I cast out demons by the finger of God, then the kingdom of God has come upon you" (Luke 11:20). Thus, Jesus saw his ministry of demon exorcisms as evidence that God's royal rule had broken into the present. By casting out demons Jesus broke the power of sin, paving the way for the restoring work of God's mission.

The followers of John the Baptist came to Jesus after their teacher was thrown into prison. They asked if he (Jesus) was the messianic agent of the kingdom. In response, Jesus pointed to his ministry of miracles. Jesus offered the fact that the blind saw, the lame walked, lepers were cleansed, the deaf heard, and the dead were raised as evidence of the kingship of God. These same kingdom signs were foretold by Isaiah and were present in Jesus' own ministry (Matt. 11:4-6; Luke 7:20-23; Isa. 35:4-6). Jesus understood these acts of ministry as evidence that the royal rule of God was a blessed present reality. In this way Jesus carried out the mission of God in the world now and not simply as a future hope. Jesus also knew that not everyone understood his miracles in this way. When asked by the Pharisees when the kingdom was coming, Jesus answered, "The kingdom of God does not come with the observation of signs, nor will they say, 'Behold, it is here or there.' For behold, the kingdom of God is among you" (Luke 17:20-21). Thus, regardless of how others understood his miracles, Jesus consistently spoke of the kingdom as a present reality.

THE KINGDOM IS FUTURE

Alongside this emphasis on the present reality of the kingdom, Jesus also taught that the kingdom was still future. In some contexts, the kingdom seemed to be in the very near future. An example is Jesus' statement, "Truly I say to you that there are some who are standing here who will not taste death until they see the kingdom of God having come in power" (Mark 9:1). In a series of parables (Matt. 24:45—25:46), Jesus portrayed the kingdom as coming in the future at a time that could not be known. The parable of the ten virgins (25:1-13) and the parable of the talents (vv. 14-30) suggest that the coming of the kingdom will be delayed long into the future. As a result those who should be ready and longing for its arrival will be distracted and thus surprised when the kingdom suddenly does come.

THE KINGDOM AS BOTH PRESENT AND FUTURE

How do we deal with the clear teaching of Jesus that the kingdom became present in his ministry, but also that the kingdom is a future reality? Certainly, Jesus believed the kingdom was both present and future. The parable comparing the kingdom to a mustard seed (Matt. 13:31-32; Mark 4:30-32; Luke 13:18-19) suggests at least two truths. One is that the kingdom is present in some real, but small measure. Second, is that its greatest expression still lies in the future. The parable of the wheat and the weeds (Matt. 13:24-30) teaches that the kingdom is a present reality. This can be seen in the young wheat sprouted from the seed sown (by Jesus). However, this parable also teaches a future reality for the kingdom. A future judgment separating the wheat and the weeds will bring the kingdom to its consummation.

Jesus did not seem concerned by the paradox that the kingdom could be both present and future. That issue occupied twentieth-century Jesus scholarship, producing a wide variety of interpretations. Perhaps the most helpful is that which saw Jesus' teachings of a present and future kingdom as a tension between the already and the not yet aspects of the kingdom. (This paradox is explored more fully in chapter 11.) The already and not yet character of the kingdom also suggests the intertwining roles of the mission of Jesus and the mission of the church in the mission of God. Through his earthly ministry Jesus inaugurated the kingdom and gave the clearest possible expression of the mission of God. But God's mission was not fully accomplished by the earthly ministry of Jesus. Through Christ, God has commissioned the church to incarnate his mission of restoring creation to its original purposes. But the final accomplishment of that mission of God will come about through the consummation of the kingdom when Christ becomes all in all.

THE KINGDOM IMPLIES A NEW ETHIC

Jesus also pointed to the mission of God by providing a new ethic for the kingdom. Nowhere is this clearer than in the Sermon on the Mount where the kingdom is characterized by the grace of God and by the expectation of obedient human response. Unfortunately, the Beatitudes often have been understood as requirements for entrance into the kingdom.

Instead, they *should* be understood as effective words of blessing to those in great need. Matthew 5:3 does not call on the religious to manufacture poverty of spirit to participate in the kingdom. Rather, that beatitude speaks the blessings of God's royal rule into reality in the lives of those whose spirits are impoverished to the point of hopelessness. Matthew 5:4 does not call either the righteous or the self-righteous to grieve their many spiritual failures. Rather, through this beatitude Jesus spoke the comforting presence of God into the aching hearts of those grieving because life (and death) has taken from them all to which they have clung. The Beatitudes forever place the ethics of the kingdom in the context of God's generous and unwavering grace extended to those in need.

The so-called Great Antitheses found in Matthew 5:21-48 illustrate kingdom grace. Consistently Jesus quoted a legal requirement from the Old Testament with the words, "You have heard it said." He then followed the quotation with "but I say to you," and revealed the heart intention of God in giving the Law. Jesus invited his followers to move from the letter of the law to find the Law's fullest meaning in graceful obedience empowered by Christ. Living up to the ethics of the kingdom as taught by Jesus is more demanding than the expectations of the other Jewish teachers of his day. Jesus taught, "Unless your righteousness abounds beyond that of the scribes and Pharisees, you will certainly not enter the kingdom of heaven" (v. 20).

But the greater righteousness demanded by kingdom ethics does not come from trying harder. Matthew 6:1-18 rejects acts of righteousness performed out of human ability for human praise. Instead, Jesus invites his followers into a life of compassion, worship, and commitment. The ability to enter such a life comes through relationship with the God who gives us our daily bread and forgives us our trespasses. As the sermon reached Matthew 6:33, Jesus promised that those who seek God's kingdom first will be blessed by having all their needs met. Matthew 7:7-11 shows that God's grace enables disciples to obey the great expectations of complete kingdom obedience. Jesus invites his followers to ask, seek, and knock, promising that God will generously give good things to those who ask him. Within the flow of the sermon, these good things certainly include the ability to live up to the ethical vision of the kingdom.

A person easily can become overwhelmed by the kingdom expectations outlined in the Sermon on the Mount. This is especially true when we assume that we must muster the moral fiber to live up to these expectations in our own strength. If we think about the kingdom ethics described in the sermon, Jesus is the only one whose life and ministry fully embodied these kingdom expectations. It is also clear that by faith and grace we are called to grow in our ability to live obediently in this kingdom way. As we do, the mission of God to restore creation to God's purposes will be accomplished in our lives. Such obedience will advance God's purposes in the lives of those with whom we interact.

THE KINGDOM IMPLIES A NEW COMMUNITY

These aspects of Jesus' teaching of the kingdom make it clear that God's royal rule is not simply a matter of individual piety. Jesus' teaching of kingdom implies a new community in which God's creation purposes for human beings can flourish. This corporate context for the kingdom is evident in many ways in Jesus' ministry and teachings. The selection of the disciples "to be with him" (Mark 3:14) indicates Jesus' purpose in building a community. That he chose twelve suggests his purpose was and is the reconstitution of Israel. The establishment of what we now call the Lord's Supper confirmed this when Jesus described the cup as "the blood of the new covenant" (Luke 22:20; 1 Cor. 11:25).

Christian history details a long and unfortunate record of arrogant Christian treatment of Jewish people. However, the community Jesus formed did not mean the rejection of old Israel nor its replacement with the church as the eternally elect people of God. It is clear in Jesus' ministry that the new community he was forming was not a replacement of Israel. It was the restoration of the people of God to the purposes for which God had called them. That is to say, Jesus' kingdom teaching implies a new community that is a foretaste of the restoration God intends for all creation.

CONCLUSION

Jesus' teaching of the royal rule of God lays out the agenda of God's mission in the world. From a Wesleyan perspective, Jesus' teaching of the kingship of God is neither speculative nor dismissive, neither other-world-ly nor simply secular. It provides a way of understanding the integration of worship with compassionate ministry, of theological reflection with social justice ministries. Matthew 5:48, "Therefore, you will be perfect as your Father in heaven is perfect," lies at the heart of the Sermon on the Mount. For this reason Jesus' ethics of the kingdom point the way to the life of holiness Wesley envisioned. Best of all, Jesus' invitation to enter the kingdom offers his church a way to participate in God's great mission. We can share in God's work to restore all creation to the purposes for which God originally created it.

6
MISSIONAL FROM FIRST TO LAST
PAUL'S LETTERS AND THE *MISSIO DEI*
Andy Johnson

═══════════════════ ◆ ═══════════════════

ISRAEL AND THE *MISSIO DEI*

In the beginning of the Bible's story, God created humanity in God's own image for the purpose of reflecting God's gracious rule over creation. If humans would do this, all creation would reach its full potential, flourishing with well-ordered life (Gen. 1:28; 2:15). Rather than fulfilling this charge, Adam and Eve, though created in God's image, succumbed to the temptation to "be like God" (3:5). They therefore overstepped their creaturely bounds and exploited their status as God's image-bearers. As a result, creation became susceptible to the power of sin and death, and our first parents ended up alienated from God (v. 8), from each other (vv. 12, 16), and even from God's good creation (vv. 15, 17-19). With its power unleashed, sin "lurk[ed] at [Cain's] door" (4:7), stimulating evil, violence, and death, all of which served to strengthen sin's power (vv. 1-16; 6:5-6, 11-12). Even after the flood, humans still were inclined toward these death-dealing forces (8:21).

Genesis 12 to Revelation 22 tells the story of God's life-giving mission to reverse all this. Saving people from the guilt they incur for their sinful actions is a part of that mission, but only part. God's larger purpose is to heal and transform people, reconciling them to him, to one another, and to God's good creation. In other words, God is on a mission to right everything that is wrong, for the purpose of bringing human beings and the rest of creation to full potential. But God did not choose to "go it alone," as it were. Rather, God chose to bless Abraham and his family and in so doing they became God's agents for bringing blessing to the world (Gen. 12:3).

After an interval of slavery in Egypt, God redeemed this (now much larger) family in the Exodus. At Sinai God set Israel apart to be a holy kingdom of priests who would reflect God's character to the rest of the world in the way they lived their life together (Exod. 19:3-6). By living in faithfulness to the covenant, they were to be a light to the nations (Isa. 42:6), a "showcase" or model for the way God had created humans to live. They were to be the instrument through which God would reestablish God's reign over a world gone awry, bringing forgiveness of sins, reconciliation among the nations, and peace and healing to his creation. Unfortunately, Israel often failed to confront the idolatrous way of life of the surrounding nations and, instead, was absorbed into it. Though Israel failed, God was faithful, sending prophet after prophet to call them back to their role in God's mission (Jer. 4:1-2).

Paul on the Plight of God's Creation

By Paul's day, the Jewish people were not explicitly engaged in worshipping idols. But in Paul's view, Israel as a whole still had not been faithful to their calling (Rom. 3:1-3; 9:4-6). The world was enslaved by the powers of sin and death unleashed by Adam's disobedience (5:12-14). People were alienated from God (v. 10) and from one another (Jew from Gentile, nation from nation, as in Eph. 2:14). Paul even spoke of the whole creation groaning in its enslavement to the corrupting influence of sin and death (Rom 8:19-22). He was clear that individuals commit sinful acts (3:23). However, when Paul spoke of people being under the power of sin or enslaved to it (6:15-23), he personified sin. This is sin with a capital "S," a harsh master (compare Gen. 4:7), a cosmic power. Sin in this sense clearly is related to individual sinful acts, but this sin is more than simply the sum of all of your sins and mine. Moreover, the result of this sin is death, with a capital "D."

Sin and death in this larger sense are at work in severely dysfunctional families where domestic violence characterizes one generation after another. The violence some children experience every day actually gets hardwired into the neural networks of their brain. This shapes them into thinking that violence is the normal way of dealing with family life. Not surprisingly, when they become spouses and parents, their natural inclination is often to continue this cycle, inflicting violence on family members. They certainly do need to be reconciled to God. But that is not sufficient remedy for the situation. They also need to be reconciled with those who have treated them violently, and with those they have treated violently. As pastors who deal with these situations regularly know, not only do such people need to have their own mind-sets transformed, their network of family relationships needs to be transformed as well. They need to be liberated from the power of sin and death that drives the whole cycle of generational violence.

Sin as an enslaving power is at work in drug and alcohol abuse, in pornography, and in the poverty that leaves a young woman thinking abortion is her only option. Sin is at work in the gang violence in our urban areas that catches up many young men into its endless retaliation, landing many of them in prison or the grave. Sin's power is at work in more "respectable" ways too, as when advertising media shape us into consumers ("coveters" would be a more accurate description) who *must* have the latest and best toys. Sin is at work in the pillaging of God's good creation when the injustice of global poverty moves villagers to strip their land of trees that hold crop-producing soil in place. This results in erosion, worse poverty, hunger, and often the violence of endless civil wars. And on it goes. For Paul, sin is an enslaving power that fuels individual sinful acts that, in turn, feed sin and make it even more powerful. This eventually leads persons, societies, and even God's good creation itself into the waiting arms of death.

But God has invaded the world he loves to rescue it from sin and death by graciously sending his Son as Israel's Messiah, in faithfulness both to Israel and to the world. We now turn to look more closely at God's faithful action.

JESUS' MISSION ACCORDING TO PAUL

Paul's letters help us understand how Jesus' mission relates to God's overall mission and what that means for the mission of God's people. One place where this comes into focus is in the way Paul tells Jesus' story in Philippians 2:6-11. This may have been a hymn sung by early Christians, and in it we see the basic shape of Jesus' mission and the final goal toward which it is directed. Paul begins by describing Jesus as one

who, although he was in the form of God, did not consider this equality with God as something to be exploited. Rather, he poured himself out by taking the form of a slave, by being born in the likeness of human beings. And being found in human form, he humbled himself by becoming obedient all the way to death—even death on a cross.

Therefore God has indeed highly exalted him and granted to him the name that is above every name. God did this so that at this name belonging to Jesus every knee should bow in heaven, and on earth, and under the earth, and every tongue confess that Jesus, the Messiah, is Lord, leading to the glory of God the Father.*

In this passage, Paul says that Jesus was equal with God, God in visible form. However, unlike Adam and Eve who grasped at godlike status, Jesus refused to exploit his status of (already) being equal to God. Instead, he emptied himself, lowering his status by taking the form of a slave and becoming fully human. In doing so, he was faithfully obedient in carrying out God's missional intent, whereas Adam and ancient Israel were not. Jesus revealed the essence of what God intended for Israel and for all humans—faithful obedience to God the Father expressed in self-giving love for others. In this same act, he revealed the essence of God's own character as one who displays his power precisely through his vulnerable love. Jesus showed the lengths to which God would go to carry out his life-giving mission, even to the point of becoming human in Jesus, sharing in the plight of his creation gone awry and headed down to death. Jesus' mission, then, was the means by which God carried out his life-giving mission.

Paradoxically, the flourishing life God had covenanted to give to all creation through Israel came only through death, the faithful death of his Son. God's saving covenant faithfulness ("righteousness") to Israel is revealed in Jesus' own faithfulness (Rom. 3:21-22).[1] Empowered by the Spirit, Jesus took Israel's missional place by exhibiting fidelity to God. As

---

*All Scripture quotations in this chapter are the translation of the chapter author, except where noted.

God's faithful agent he brought healing and reconciliation (5:10-11; 2 Cor. 5:17-19) and initiated God's coming reign (1 Cor. 15:24-28). In raising Jesus from the dead and highly exalting him, the Father, through the Spirit, vindicated him. This confirmed his identity as Messiah and Lord and that Jesus' mission was God's own mission (Rom. 1:4; Phil. 2:9).

The goal of this mission is expressed in Philippians 2:10-11. That goal is that every creature will bow the knee to the one true human, the incarnate Son, who will reestablish and exercise God's lordship over creation. This public confession of Jesus' lordship will occur in such a way that the proper honor ultimately will come to God the Father, the Creator of all. The picture is that of creation rectified or rightly ordered. Then God's creatures will no longer be enslaved to idols of their own making, nor to the power of sin enforced upon them by their own idolatry (reversing Rom. 1:20-23). Christ's royal coming, therefore, will achieve the final goal of God's mission, to reclaim and reestablish God's loving sovereignty over his world and to bring creation to its full potential. This is nothing short of the new creation Paul believed God already had begun to bring about through Jesus (2 Cor. 5:17; Gal. 6:15).

For Paul, then, God's own mission to establish his kingdom and bring about a new creation was carried out through Jesus. But, as with Israel in the Old Testament, Paul was convinced God wanted to form a "display people" who would publicly showcase the kingdom and the new creation now begun. Only now it was to be composed of both Jews and people from all the nations publicly giving proper honor to God together (Rom. 15:1-13; Gal. 3:29). Various saving benefits of God's mission through Jesus make the formation of a people like this possible. These benefits that come through Jesus' mission overlap. They include: (1) adoption into God's family (4:5-7; Rom. 8:15-17); (2) deliverance from cosmic powers (Gal. 4:3, 8-9; Col. 1:13) and from the idolatrous mind-set of the "present evil age" (Gal. 1:4; Rom. 12:1-2); (3) forgiveness of sins (3:25; 4:7; Col. 1:14) and liberation from sin's mastery (Rom. 6:6-7); (4) justification (4:25; 5:1, 9, 16); (5) reconciliation of us to him and to one another (2 Cor. 5:18-21; Rom. 5:1-11; Eph. 2:11-22).[2] While individual persons experience these benefits, they all take place "in Christ," that is, in the publicly visible body of Christ called the church.[3] It is this whole people whom God has called or elected *in Christ* to be his showcase people, displaying God's kingdom/new creation.

1 THESSALONIANS:
ELECT FOR PARTICIPATION IN GOD'S MISSION

Paul often spoke of God's first action on behalf of his converts as a "calling" (*klēsis*),[4] a word closely related both to "election" (*eklogē*) and "church" (*ekklēsia*). Early on in 1 Thessalonians, Paul gave thanks for the church because, as he said, "We know God has elected *you all*" (1:4). Paul was not saying God had arbitrarily predestined each of these *individuals* for salvation. Rather, he used plural language in speaking about God's choosing the church *as a whole people*. His words reflect Old Testament language about God choosing Israel *as a whole* as an instrument in his saving mission (Ps. 105:6; Isa. 41:8-10; 42:1; 49:1-7). In the following verses (1 Thess. 1:5-8), Paul gave the reasons he knew God had elected this church for participating in his mission: (1) because of the powerful way the Spirit-empowered proclamation of the gospel had come to them (v. 5); and (2) because the church body as a whole had become a public model,[5] showcasing their believing allegiance ("faith") to God, in spite of extreme social and political pressures (vv. 6-8; 2:14; 3:3).

In verse 6, Paul said the church had become "imitators of us and of the Lord." Paul had told them about Jesus' faithfulness to God and self-giving actions toward others in carrying out God's mission. They had also seen this pattern of life modeled by Paul (2:1-12). Now, they too, enabled by the Spirit, were modeling this life pattern in Thessalonica (1:3, 6, 8-10; 4:9-10). Verse 8 fleshes this out, "For from you *the message about the Lord* has rung out not only in Macedonia and Achaia. But in every place *your faithfulness to God* has gone forth." That is, not only had their oral proclamation[6] about God's mission in Jesus reverberated throughout the region, but also had their own faithful pattern of life. Speaking about the Lord's saving mission goes hand in hand with an observable pattern of life that reflects that mission.

To be clear, in verse 8 Paul did not say their "inner" faith *resulted in* public faithfulness. Rather, this sort of faith was, *by definition,* an observable (and costly) turning away from society's idols to serve God exclusively as they waited faithfully for Jesus' royal coming (vv. 9-10). This church provided a public witness together, with both their words and their life pattern, to the sort of life God intends for everyone. Their life together resembled the final goal of God's mission because their posture/life pattern ("bent knees") and words ("confessing tongues") gave public witness that the crucified and vindicated Jesus is Lord. They were "walking worthily of the God who [was] calling" all of them together "into his kingdom and glory" (2:12). Their life together mirrored Jesus' own life pattern of fidelity to God and self-giving love for others (1:3, 6; 4:9-10). This is how Paul knew God had elected them—as beneficiaries of God's mission in Christ, they now were participating in that mission.

A Concluding Word

The church is set apart by the Spirit to mirror God's final goal for creation. As such the Spirit enables it to become conformed to the image of Christ (Rom. 8:29) as a channel of God's saving activity. For example, the church's very identity is that we are those who have been reconciled to God through Christ. As a reconciled people, we also are channels of God's reconciling activity. Through the Spirit, we are to be "reconciled reconcilers" (2 Cor. 5:18-21). We have been "justified," "set right," through God's righteousness/justice revealed in Jesus' faithfulness (Rom. 3:21-22; 5:1). God's righteousness is the saving activity God displayed in Jesus that demonstrated his own covenant faithfulness. We are, then, to be channels of God's saving activity that makes things right or just. As Paul said, the purpose of God's work in Christ was so that "we might become God's righteousness in him" (2 Cor. 5:21). We are to be "weapons of God's righteousness/justice" (Rom. 6:13, 19)—"set-right channels of God's setting-right activity" or "justified seekers of God's justice."

The church's participation in God's mission may take many different forms depending on the ways sin as an enslaving power is at work in particular cultural situations. Where drug and alcohol abuse enslave people and wreck families, the church can provide broad-based programs to help addicts become free from these enslaving idols and reconciled to God and to their own families. In this way, the church would display its identity as "set-right channels of God's setting-right mission" and as "reconciled reconcilers."

Where sin rears its head in community disputes that become bitter and even violent, the church can work in mediating ways to help all sides come together and listen to one another. This is exactly what a Nazarene church in the Midwest did when a dispute between schoolteachers and the local school board became a bitter conflict, with sin powerfully at work dividing the community. The pastors helped their people recognize their identity as "reconciled reconcilers," and God's Spirit enabled the church to become an agent for reconciliation in their town.

Where sin takes the form of injustice that keeps some from obtaining even basic health care, a number of churches have begun parish nursing programs. These programs, literally life-giving in many communities, reflect the life-giving mission of God. Churches like these recognize their identity as "justified seekers of God's justice."

It is important to recognize that such endeavors are not add-on activities to what the church is. They are concrete ways the Spirit enables the church to fulfill its calling, to live into its identity, as it is being conformed to Christ. As God's "display people," the church exists by sharing in Jesus' missional story and reflecting his faithfulness to God and his love for others. In doing so, they thereby bear witness to God's final goal for creation. Like Paul's letters, the church's very identity is missional from first to last.

PART II
WESLEYAN THEOLOGY AND THE *MISSIO DEI*

7

THE MISSION OF THE HOLY TRINITY

Thomas A. Noble

---◆---

The doctrine of the Trinity—that God is the Father, the Son, and the Holy Spirit—is fundamental to all Christian belief. It is the most comprehensive doctrine of Christian theology. It is the first article of faith, for example, in the Nazarene Articles of Faith, as in the doctrinal statements of many denominations and parachurch organizations. But for many years (until the middle of the twentieth century) the doctrine was something of a dead letter. Even today, while Christian theologians are devoting great attention to it, lay Christians still generally do not. We say we believe it, but many of us do not really think it is of any practical relevance. What has it got to do (we may ask) with salvation or mission or the life of the church?

When you think about it, that is rather curious! If this is *who God is*—Father, Son, and Holy Spirit—should it not be intimately related to all God does? If we are to be "in the image of God," does that not mean that *who we are to be* is to be shaped and formed by *who God is*?[1]

And what about the great missionary text we call "The Great Commission"? It is about mission: "Go therefore and make disciples of all nations." But it also is about the Holy Trinity: "baptizing them in the name of the Father and of the Son and of the Holy Spirit" (Matt. 28:19).* How could we miss the close connection? Yet, sadly, some may skip this chapter because they really do not believe God the Holy Trinity has anything to do with the practicalities of mission. And for them, mission is what matters, not God!

---

*All Scripture quotations in this chapter are from the NRSV, except where noted.

77

The Latin word *missio*—from which we get the English words "mission," "missional," and "missionary"—means "a sending." In John's gospel, the equivalent of the Great Commission text at the end of Matthew's gospel, is the saying of the risen Lord, "As the Father has sent me, so I send you" (John 20:21). This too is another way of stating that the mission of the church is in fact the *missio Dei*, the mission of God. That is where we begin.

THE FATHER SENT THE SON

This is a particularly clear emphasis in John's gospel. We all can quote the "gospel in a nutshell" text, "For God so loved the world that he gave his only Son, so that everyone who believes in him may not perish but may have eternal life" (John 3:16). But the fact that the Father *sent* the Son is clear throughout the whole gospel. John 4:34 records this saying of Jesus, "My food is to do the will of him who sent me and to complete his work." At 12:49, Jesus identified him "who sent me" with the Father, saying, "For I have not spoken on my own, but the Father who sent me has himself given me a commandment about what to say and what to speak."

This also was a theme of Paul's. Before John put pen to papyrus, Paul had already written to the Galatians, "But when the fullness of time had come, God sent his Son, born of a woman, born under the law" (Gal. 4:4). God was not compelled to do that, of course, not even by his own nature. That would deny grace. The God who gave his name as "I will be who I will be" (Exod. 3:14, author's translation) graciously and lovingly willed to send his only Son.

But what did the Father send the Son to do? Briefly, he was sent to preach, to teach, and to heal, but more definitively, to *die*. Much more needs to be said about that, but we shall explore this more fully in the next chapter. Meanwhile we must move on to another aspect of the mission of God—the Holy Trinity. For not only did the Father send the Son to die for our salvation, but also the Father and the Son together sent the Holy Spirit.

THE FATHER AND THE SON SENT THE SPIRIT

It cannot be said that the Spirit ever was absent from the world. Christians read Genesis 1:2 as referring to the work of the Spirit in cre-

ation, and clearly the Spirit was active throughout the era of the old covenant, anointing kings and priests. He also "spoke by the prophets" (as the creed puts it), preparing the way for the One who was to come. According to the Gospels, the Spirit was also at work in the sending of the Son, for his human birth was effected by action of the Spirit, moving again over the waters, this time in the womb of Mary (Matt. 1:20; Luke 1:35).

Not only so, but throughout the ministry of Jesus, the Spirit was active. He came down upon Jesus in a new way at his baptism (Luke 3:22) so that Jesus was "full of the Holy Spirit" (4:1). Jesus was led by the Spirit into the wilderness to undergo severe temptation before returning in "the power of the Spirit" to Galilee (v. 14). There he began his ministry by reading from the scroll of the prophet Isaiah, "The Spirit of the Lord is upon me" (v. 18).

But the Gospels also make clear that the Spirit, while never absent, was to be sent in a new way. All three Synoptic Gospels report John the Baptist's prophecy that Jesus was the one who would "baptize . . . with the Holy Spirit" (Matt. 3:11; Mark 1:8; Luke 3:16). In John's gospel the link between Jesus' baptism with the Spirit and the later baptism of his disciples is particularly clear. The Baptist reported, "I myself did not know him, but the one who sent me to baptize with water said to me, 'He on whom you see the Spirit descend and remain is the one who baptizes with the Holy Spirit'" (John 1:33). Jesus as a human being received the Holy Spirit at his baptism, and (unlike the occasional coming of the Spirit before then), the Spirit *remained* on him in order that he should give the Spirit to us "without measure" (3:34).

This new coming of the Spirit had to wait until Jesus was "glorified" through his death and resurrection (7:39). In the farewell discourses of John 14—16, Jesus spoke several times of this new sending of the Spirit. At 14:16, he said he would ask the Father, and he would send *another* Paraclete, "to be with you forever."[2] Jesus is the Paraclete, our "advocate with the Father," according to 1 John 2:1; the Spirit is *another* Paraclete. We might say the Spirit is the *alter ego* of Jesus. Again at John 14:26, Jesus spoke of the Paraclete as, "the Holy Spirit, whom the Father will send in my name." Jesus would ask, and the Father would send the Spirit in his name. At 15:26, Jesus stated it a little differently, "When the [Paraclete] comes, whom I will send to you from the Father, the Spirit of truth who comes from the Father, he will testify on my behalf." This time, the exalted Lord Jesus would send the Spirit, and yet there is no contradiction, for the Spirit "comes" or "proceeds" from the Father. The mission of the Spirit is to draw attention to Jesus, to "prove the world wrong about sin and righteousness and judgment" (16:8), and to lead Jesus' disciples "into all the truth" (v. 13).

In John's gospel this seems to be fulfilled after Jesus was glorified on the cross, when the newly resurrected Lord breathed on the disciples and said, "Receive the Holy Spirit" (20:22). Perhaps this is best understood as another acted parable, fulfilled on the day of Pentecost, not reported in John, but in Acts. Luke identified Pentecost as the moment when the exalted Lord baptized the apostles with the Holy Spirit, giving them "power" for mission, to witness to the Lord Jesus "in all Judea and Samaria, and to the ends of the earth" (1:8). Throughout Acts, the *Holy Spirit* empowered the mission of the church.

The mission of the New Testament church, then, is not centered on what the church does. It is about *what God already has done in the death and resurrection of the Lord Jesus.* It is not about us; it is about him. Everything else (repentance, forgiveness, a new life of holiness, acts of compassion) follows from that. The *imperatives* (Repent! Believe! Go!) follow from the *indicatives,* the statements of what God *has done* by his Spirit in the life, death, and resurrection of the Lord Jesus. That is why preaching, specifically the preaching of the gospel, is the heart of the mission of the church. The book of Acts, with the New Testament as a whole, makes it clear that only when the church focuses first and foremost on evangelism, the proclamation of the gospel, is its mission truly the *missio Dei.* Our word "evangelism" itself comes from the Greek verb *euangelizomai,* to proclaim or announce the good (*eu*) news or message (*angelion*). This gospel comes "not in word only, but also in power and in the Holy Spirit" (1 Thess. 1:5). *Because* the Father and the Son have sent the Spirit, the church may participate in the mission of God.

THE SENDING/COMING TRINITY

[handwritten: character of God is central]

So far we have traced the sending of the Son by the Father and the sending of the Spirit by the Father and the Son. But this story of the New Testament leaves some unanswered questions we must face.

It is possible to speak of "God" sending his Son and his Spirit and yet not be clear about who it is to whom this word "God" refers. If these are three "persons" (as the language of the church, though not of the New Testament, puts it), does that mean they are three individuals? If so, we may conclude that only the Father is "God"; the Son and the Spirit whom he sends are not God. That obviously is not acceptable, for both Son and Spirit are acknowledged as God in the New Testament. It would also mean that God the Father sat unaffected, enjoying the glory of heaven, but sent another individual to do his dirty work. But who would this sent individual be, if he is not God? Some archangel? That would be a denial of the gospel of the love of God. If God is not prepared to come to the rescue in person, how can we claim that this demonstrates that God loves us? The deity of Christ and of the Spirit are essential to the gospel and to the *missio Dei*.

Even that does not answer fully. It still leaves the possibility that these persons are three separate individuals, each of whom is God. That would be tritheism, the doctrine of three gods. Not only does that fly in the face of Israel's great confession, endorsed by Jesus, "Hear, O Israel: the Lord our God, the Lord is one" (Mark 12:29, quoting Deut. 6:4). This, again, would mean God the Father sent another god, God the Son, to suffer on our behalf. Both are unacceptable. We are driven to one conclusion: Father, Son, and Holy Spirit are not three gods, but one God. God may be three persons, but there are not three individuals. The triune God must be confessed to be one individual, one God in three persons, three persons in one indivisible God.

The word "individual" means "an indivisible unity," and that is who our God is. It is a theological error to speak of three parts or members of the Trinity. (Even some theologians slip into that error!) The formative theologians of this doctrine were Athanasius and the three Cappadocian fathers—Basil of Caesarea, Gregory of Nazianzus, and Gregory of Nyssa. Their Trinitarian theology asserts that God is wholly the Father and the

Father is wholly God; God is <u>wholly</u> the Son and the Son is wholly God; God is wholly the Spirit, and the Spirit is wholly God. Gregory of Nazianzus, the theologian of the Trinity par excellence, suggested the helpful illustration that, just as in mathematics, <u>three infinities</u> add up to one infinity, so in God the three distinct but inseparable persons are one God. Not only is the Father "God," but also the Son and the Holy Spirit. "When I say God," he declared, "I mean Father, Son and Holy Spirit."[3]

The <u>implications</u> of this for the *missio Dei* are immense. We will mention three, briefly.

①   *First,* we cannot think of the Father dictating to an <u>unwilling</u> Son and an unwilling Spirit. The expression, "God so loved the world that he gave his only Son" (John 3:16), must be taken to imply that *God the Holy Trinity*—the Father, the Son, and the Holy Spirit—so loved the world. Indeed, we must affirm paradoxically that not only the Father, but also the Son and the Holy Spirit in unity with the Father, sent the Son and the Spirit. The <u>triune</u> God is the <u>sending</u> God.

②   *Second,* we cannot think of the Son coming on his own in such a way that he is separated from the Father and the Spirit. Only the Son became incarnate, died on the cross, and was raised from the dead. But all during "the days of his flesh" (Heb. 5:7), the Son was in the Father and the Father was in the Son (John 17:21) in the unity of the Holy Spirit. By the Holy Spirit, in a way we cannot fathom, the Father was with and in the Son even as he hung on the cross. Even when abandoned by the Father while he hung on the cross (Mark 15:34), a separation that speaks of the reality of the evil they had to overcome, paradoxically we have to say (with Jürgen Moltmann) that the Father and the Son were united by the Holy Spirit in their common purpose of love for each other and for the world. All this means the *sending* God is also the <u>sent</u> God.

③   *Third,* the church has <u>no mission of its own.</u> Rather, the church is caught up in the power of the Spirit in the mission of God. The "acts of the Holy Spirit" continue, and the acts of the Holy Spirit are the acts of the Son. Even though gone from us into the nearer presence of the Father, the risen Lord is with us in the power of his Spirit, even "to the end of the age" (Matt. 28:20). And if the Spirit and the Son are with us in mission, so too is the Father. Consequently, we may pray, "Our Father," knowing he hears us.

Moreover, since the Spirit of the Son, the Spirit of adoption, indwells us, we too may say, along with him, "Abba, Father!"

Conclusion: Mission Is Not the End

This brings us finally to an important conclusion: the *missio Dei* is not the End. To put it another way, the End will end the mission. Continuing the *missio Dei* is not the *ultimate* purpose of God, so mission is not the *ultimate* purpose of the church. At the End, the *eschaton,* the end of "the present evil age" (Gal. 1:4), the mission will be completed. In one sense, it is completed already (John 19:30). Jesus has made "for all time" (Heb. 10:14) what the *Book of Common Prayer* (so loved by Wesley) calls the one "full, perfect, and sufficient sacrifice, oblation, and satisfaction, for the sins of the whole world." In another sense, the mission of the Son through the Spirit continues to the end of the age, to put that salvation into effect throughout the world.

But at the end of the age, the *missio Dei* will end. It will be completed. That is vitally important; it means that while mission is an integral part of the nature of the church in this age, it is not what ultimately makes the church, the church. The church still will be the church, the body of Christ, in the age to come. The salvation of the world through the *missio Dei* is therefore the *penultimate purpose* of the church. The *ultimate* purpose of the church is *the glory of God*.   Penultimate v. Ultimate purpose

Within the conditions of this age then, the church lives in a twofold movement. There is not only the outward scattering movement of the *missio Dei,* the mission of evangelism and compassion, but also the returning, gathering movement of worship. That too has to be seen in Trinitarian context. Not only does the Father send the Son, and the Father and Son send the Spirit, but also the Son glorifies the Father (John 17:1, 4) and the Spirit glorifies the Son (16:14). Not only is the movement of the *missio Dei* downward and outward from the Father through the Son in the Holy Spirit, but there is also the returning, gathering movement by the Spirit through the Son to the Father, whose goal and end is the *gloria Dei.*[4] *Worship* is the *ultimate* purpose of the church.

When we obey the Great Commission, then, and *go,* we do so to say, "Come." And the call to come is the call to be baptized *into* the one name of the inseparable Father, Son, and Holy Spirit (never one without the other). The call is to become one of the people of God, his *called ones,* his c*alled out* ones, his *called together* ones, his *ecclesia,* his church. These *two* directions are essential to being the church, at least within this present evil age—the *going out* in mission, and the c*oming together* in worship and fellowship. These are the *diastole* and the *systole* at the heart of the church in this present age.   Go out + come together

The great Missionary himself set the tone, "*Come* to me, all you who are weary and burdened, and I will give you rest" (Matt. 11:28, NIV, emphasis added). The gospel is a proclamation—what God *has done* in his Son—issuing in an invitation, a *call,* "Ho, everyone who thirsts, come to the waters; and you that have no money, come, buy and eat! Come, buy wine and milk without money and without price" (Isa. 55:1). So we sing our songs of *invitation:* "You that are troubled and burdened by sin, *come* just as you are"; "*Come,* every one who is thirsty in spirit, *Come* every one who is weary and sad"; "*Come home, come home,* You who are weary, *come home.*"

The mission is not ours. It is the mission of God the Holy Trinity—the Father sending the Son, then the Father and the Son sending the Spirit. But the returning movement, the *ecclesia,* the gathering of the people of God, is similarly Trinitarian, for by the one Spirit we are united to the one Son, and in the one Son we offer ourselves in praise and worship to the "one God and Father of all, who is above all and through all and in all" (Eph. 4:6). Mission is not then an end in itself. The purpose of mission is the gathering of all, uniting in the one, holy, catholic, and apostolic church (1:10, 22-23) to the glory of our Trinitarian God. *Soli deo gloria.*

Purpose of mission

8

KENŌSIS
THE MISSION OF THE SON
Thomas A. Noble

════════════════════ ◆ ════════════════════

The previous chapter was devoted to the wide and comprehensive view of the *missio Dei* as the mission of God the Holy Trinity. Within that scope, we gave some attention to the specific mission of the Son, but much more needs to be said about that. For example, we noted that repeatedly in the gospel of John, Jesus speaks of being "sent" by the Father, but we did not really address in any depth the question of what the Father sent him to do. Briefly (we said), he was sent to preach, to teach, and to heal, but more definitively, to *die.* Here, we need to begin by unpacking the meaning and implications of that sentence.

SENT TO PREACH, TO TEACH, TO HEAL

Quite clearly, the Father sent the Son to *preach* and *teach*. His *preaching* was the proclamation of the coming kingdom or "rule" of God. The Greek word for proclamation, *kērygma,* is related to the word *kēryx,* meaning "herald." Jesus was the herald of the kingdom of God. But more than that, his proclamation not only foretold the coming of God's effective rule but actually effected it. In the life and ministry of Jesus, God *already* ruled. In the flesh and mind and heart of this man, the rule of God already was embodied.

Therefore, Jesus not only was the *kēryx* of the kingdom but also was the *didaskalos,* the teacher or rabbi, who gave his authoritative *didache* (teaching). "You have heard that it was said to those of ancient times . . . , but I say to you . . ." (Matt. 5:21-22).* At the end of the Sermon on the

---

*All Scripture quotations in this chapter are from the NRSV, except where noted.

Mount, Matthew commented, "The crowds were astounded at his teaching, for he taught them as one having authority, and not as their scribes" (7:28-29). Where did his authoritative teaching come from? Going back to the gospel of John, the saying at John 12:49 makes this explicit; the Father who sent Jesus gave him "what to say and what to speak." This is equally clear at 7:16, "My teaching is not mine but his who sent me"; see also the following verses.

Not only the great *words* of Jesus but also the great *works* of Jesus are those which the Father sent him to do, "The works that the Father has given me to complete, the very works that I am doing, testify on my behalf that the Father has sent me" (John 5:36). This saying is part of an extended passage in which Jesus linked his mission as the Son with the authoritative sending of the Father, and it comes right after the healing of the invalid man by the pool of Bethesda.

So not only the preaching and teaching of Jesus, but also his ministry of healing, are part of what the Father sent him to do. Jesus is not merely some kind of Greek philosopher who brings wise teaching about abstract truth or makes insightful comments (like the ancient school of wandering philosophers known as the Cynics). He *does* truth: he enacts truth. He not only preaches and teaches but also heals. His ministry includes physical salvation. The accounts of his ministry in the Synoptic Gospels make it clear that he also brings *psychic* salvation. Along with many other exorcisms, the healing of the demoniac, which resulted in the deranged and dangerous man sitting down with Jesus "clothed and in his right mind" (Mark 5:15), is a sign that healing of mind as well as body was an integral part of what the Father sent the Son to do.

One of the great pioneer Nazarene missionaries, David Hynd of Swaziland, took as his motto text Matthew 9:35, "Then Jesus went about all the cities and villages, teaching in their synagogues, and proclaiming the good news of the kingdom, and curing every disease and every sickness." The mission of the Son, given to him by the Father, was to teach, to *preach,* and to *heal.* Consequently, in all the outstations round the great mission station at Manzini, David Hynd built a church, a school, and a clinic, physically embodying the threefold ministry of Jesus. If we are to be involved in the *missio Dei* as it was embodied in the incarnate

Son, then also for us, preaching, teaching, and healing must be the three dimensions of mission. Only when we preach the gospel that alone gives the sure hope of the coming of the kingdom in glory and power, and teach the implications for our lives and practices today, and engage in the healing of people and communities sick in body and mind, can we be engaged in the mission of Jesus.

But there is more. If we stop there, then we might think the Son was sent only to make us better informed, to make life more pleasant and bearable, to give us hope, and to engage in social reform to produce a just society. We *have* to say more.

THE FATHER SENT THE SON TO DIE

The mission of the Son was not just to teach, to preach, and to heal. It was to die. Here we come to the great mystery. Teaching, preaching, and healing seem so positive. We can understand that. But to die? Did the Father really send the Son to die?

Here we must begin with the great saying of Jesus himself, "The Son of Man came not to be served but to serve, and to give his life a ransom for many" (Mark 10:45). It is clear from all four Gospels that Jesus saw his death as the will of the Father. Therefore, his death was not senseless or meaningless; it was a purposeful, intentional death. A ransom (*lutron*) is that which "redeems"; the root meaning of "redemption" (*apolutrosis*) is "to release," "to set free" (*apoluō*). Jesus' death somehow *redeems* us— sets us free!

It is quite clear Jesus was not speaking just of release from physical or social slavery. In the acted parable of the Last Supper, Jesus explained the meaning of his death as he handed the disciples the cup, "Drink from it, all of you; for this is my blood of the covenant, which is poured out for many for the forgiveness of sins" (Matt. 26:27-28). Jesus' death somehow redeems us from sin and condemnation, and reconciles us to God in the new covenant. In the language attributed to Jesus often in John's gospel, he came to be "lifted up" (glorified on the cross!) in order that we may not "perish" but receive "eternal life." Jesus died that we may live![1]

But we need to put this in broader perspective, for while the focus is on the cross, many have understood the atonement in a very hard-

and-fast legal way because they have not looked at it in the context of the *whole* mission of Jesus. To gain some true understanding of the mystery of Christ's atonement, we have to set it in the context of the whole story of his coming, and nowhere in the New Testament is that done more comprehensively than in the famous words of what scholars call the "Christological Hymn" of Philippians 2:6-11. Many scholars (though not all) think Paul was quoting here from a hymn or poem already known to the Philippians; whether it is a quotation or Paul's own composition does not matter in the end.

KENŌSIS (emptying)

Paul introduced the hymn with the words, "Let the same mind [disposition, intention] be in you that was in Christ Jesus" (v. 5). Clearly, he was calling the Philippian Christians, and us, to imitate Christ. We are to be like him. But the hymn then begins with the way in which we are not like him! Jesus was "in the form of God" (v. 6). The Greek word *morphe,* which is accurately translated "form," rather than "nature," indicates what a thing *is.* Despite his status as God, however, he did not regard this equality with God as something to be "grasped" (NIV) or "exploited." Instead of clinging to this divine status, he "emptied himself, taking the form of a slave, being born in human likeness" (v. 7). The verb "emptied" (*ekenōsen*) gives us the word *kenōsis,* meaning an "emptying."

Several points need to be clarified here. First of all, in order to be consistent with the rest of Paul's writings, the word "emptied" (*ekenōsen*) cannot be taken to mean that in order to become human, the Son ceased to be "in the form of God." His being human is added to his being God; it does not replace it. Second, the "taking the form of a slave" occurred at the same time as the self-emptying, as did the "being born in human likeness." This is one and the same act in which he simultaneously "emptied" himself, took the form (again *morphe*) of a slave, and was born in the "likeness" (*homoiōmati*) of humanity. Again, to be consistent with the rest of Paul's writings, this cannot be taken to mean that Jesus is merely "like" a human being. It asserts that he became and is a human being, which in the "Christological Hymn" is equated with being a "slave."

There is no good reason to deny that Paul referred here to that same act which John recounted as "the Word became flesh" (John 1:14). But there is a difference of emphasis. Whereas John continued, "and lived among us, and we have seen his glory," Paul spoke of this as a "self-emptying." Where John seems to have put the focus on an evident "glory" even in the human Jesus, Paul seems to be saying that the "self-emptying" means his glory was hidden. That, at any rate, is the meaning that Christian tradition has given to the concept of *kenōsis,* that by his incarnation, the glory and deity of the Son of God were hidden, concealed, or veiled.

Charles Wesley has taught us to see it that way in his Christmas hymn "Hark! The Herald Angels Sing," in the second stanza line, "Veiled in flesh, the Godhead see." That is a paradox. Somehow we "see" his Godhead or deity (the same word, *deitas,* in Greek), but that is despite the fact his glory is "veiled." Wesley repeated that emphasis in the third stanza when he interpreted the *kenōsis* with the words, "Mild, he lays his glory by." The nuancing is very subtle; even while using the words from the Johannine text, "flesh" and "glory," Wesley gave them the Pauline emphasis, the self-emptying and the hiddenness of the divine glory.

But the next verse of the Pauline hymn takes the emphasis on *kenōsis* further. Not only did Jesus "empty himself," veiling his deity, laying aside his glory in the act of becoming incarnate, but also "being found in human form [*schēmati*], he humbled himself and became obedient to the point of death—even death on a cross" (vv. 7-8).

Two things become evident here. First, there is clearly a continuity from incarnation through his incarnate life right through to his death. It is one continuous movement of self-denial. His death was not an isolated event or action of self-denial, but the culmination of the movement that began with his determination not to cling to his divine prerogatives and status. Rather, Jesus *chose* to abase himself by taking human form, which in the hymn is the "form of a slave," and to carry through this movement all the way to the ultimate self-denial in a degrading death on a Roman cross. But second, it becomes clear that this movement, this journey or downward progress from heavenly glory to excruciating death, is done in *willing* obedience. *That* is what makes it clear that this was a *missio,* a *sending.*

It has not been stated who did the sending, but Paul's "Christological Hymn" goes on to say that the consequence of this ("therefore") is that *God* exalted him (v. 9), so it is a reasonable inference that the sender is "God." The mission of self-abasement and self-denial results in his exaltation by "God" to the place of supreme sovereignty over the universe and the confession that he is the "Lord" of Israel's great confession (Deut. 6:4). But this rules out any idea that he is a second god, for not only is the divine name given to him, but this also is "to the glory of God the Father" (Phil. 2:11).

HOW DO WE PARTICIPATE IN THE MISSION OF JESUS?

What then can we say about how we are to participate in the *missio Dei* in the light of what Paul's "Christological Hymn" says about the mission of the Son?

First of all, there is that about the mission of the Son that is unique to him. We do not begin by sharing the status or form of God, and we will not be exalted to divine sovereignty over the universe. This reminds us that his cross too is unique. Paul wrote to the Corinthians that "Christ died for our sins" (1 Cor. 15:3); we are not called to repeat that. That is unique to Jesus; he was sent to do something no one else could do.

Paul wrote to the Galatians that in his death on the "tree," Christ "redeemed us from the curse of the law by becoming a curse for us" (Gal. 3:13). That too is unique to him; he took the curse that was due to us. We are not called and not able to repeat that. Jesus himself said that he came to "give his life a ransom for many" (Mark 10:45). We are not called to do that; that is unique to him. He is "the Lamb of God who takes away the sin of the world" (John 1:29). He is the one "whom God put forward as a sacrifice of atonement by his blood" (Rom. 3:25). He is the one who has "appeared once for all at the end of the age to remove sin by the sacrifice of himself" (Heb. 9:26). None of these things can be said about us. In these ways his mission was unique.

But there is a way we are called to participate in his mission. "If any want to become my followers, let them deny themselves and take up their cross and follow me" (Mark 8:34). The *kenōsis*, the self-emptying or self-

Kenōsis

denial, is not optional; it is required. That is what is meant by having the same mind, disposition, or intention as the Lord Jesus. It is the willingness to become an obedient slave to God.

Let us be clear about this. To participate in the mission of Jesus is not a matter of gaining status or position. It is not even a matter of exercising our natural abilities or our gifts of personality or intellect. It is not a matter of being a good "people person," of winning friends and influencing people, or of being a good manager, organizer, or leader. It is not even a matter of being a well-meaning philanthropist or idealist who loves humanity. In fact, these natural gifts and attitudes will be a snare as long as they are *merely* natural. Before we can receive them back as genuine gifts of the Spirit, we have to *die to our own way*, our own comfort, our own promotion, our own career prospects, the display of our own talents and personalities. The old holiness preachers used to talk about "surrender" and "total consecration," and they were dead right.

That was what *kenōsis* meant for the Son of God. The secret of his mission did not lie in his ability to preach or teach or heal. It did not lie in his divine attributes or his human compassion. It lay in his willingness to deny himself all the way to the cross, his willingness to *die.* And we can only participate in his mission if we are prepared to go with him through the garden of surrender all the way to the cross.

Only in that way can we participate in the *missio Dei*.

9

THE MISSION OF THE HOLY SPIRIT
PENTECOSTAL FELLOWSHIP
K. Steve McCormick

═══════════════ ◆ ═══════════════

WHAT IS THE MISSION OF THE HOLY SPIRIT?

The narratives of the Gospels tell the story of God's mission in such a way that wherever Jesus fulfilled the will of his Father there also was the presence of the Spirit. With every breath and step Jesus took, with every spoken word and deed, with every prayer and hope, there was the Holy Spirit faithfully guiding, teaching and illumining, inspiring and conspiring, and comforting and empowering our Lord to live in faithful resolve after the *missio Dei* through the energy of God's love. The Holy Spirit was the One who empowered Jesus to walk in the *way* of the cross while trusting in the hope and the power of the coming resurrection. The mission of the Spirit enabled Christ's faithfulness to do the will of God "on earth as . . . in heaven" (Matt. 6:10).*

As the story of God's mission is told in the concrete and unfolding scenes of the Gospels, the thread that weaves those scenes into the full tapestry of the *missio Dei* is like a riddle woven into the very fabric of the gospel. The tale of this riddle could be told as follows: *wherever the Son is, there is the Spirit, and wherever the Spirit is, there is the Son*. Whatever the Son can do, he can do only by the power of the Spirit. Whatever the Spirit can do, he can do only through the life, death, and resurrection of the Son. Whatever the Son and the Spirit do, they always do according to the character and mission of God.

Ultimately, then, according to the Gospels, the mission of Christ was fulfilled and empowered through the mission of the Spirit, and the mis-

---

*All Scripture quotations in this chapter are from the NRSV.

sion of the Spirit was fully embodied and carried out in the mission of Christ. The mission of Christ and the Spirit is always the mission of God "on earth as in heaven."   *same mission*

The mission of Christ and the Spirit comes to us wrapped in the enigma of love that "is" God. God is abundant outpouring love. The will of God in the mission of the Spirit always is to "pour out . . . on all flesh" (Joel 2:28; Acts 2:17) the abundant energy of love that is God. For in the *fullness* of God's mission, Christ and the Spirit—which the early theologian Irenaeus called the "two hands of God"—revealed that God *is* love, and that the mission of the gospel is born out of the very heart of God. Throughout the grand narrative of God's mission is this enduring riddle of condescending love: *wherever the Spirit is, there is the Son, and wherever the Son is, there is the Spirit,* the Spirit whose mission is to breathe the life, energy, and love of God on all flesh. Remember, it was by the Spirit that the Word became flesh (Luke 1:35), and it was in the flesh of humanity that Christ would bear the Spirit. Thus, all of God was with us ("Emmanuel," Matt. 1:23); "we have seen his glory . . . full of grace and truth" (John 1:14).

Given that in the mission of God it was only through the complete humanity of Christ that the Spirit was *fully* known, we may ask, then, what were some of the most pronounced and discernible ways the Spirit was always present with Christ in all the ways of God's reconciling mission? As we survey the Spirit's enduring mission we notice that it was by the Spirit, the very breath of God, that God spoke the Word that brought the creation into existence (Gen. 1; Ps. 33:9). Moreover, the Spirit of God who breathed life into Adam (Gen. 2:7) was the same life-creating, life-giving, life-sustaining Spirit who enabled Mary to conceive and give birth to the Word that is God (Matt. 1:18, 20). Amazingly, the Word that became flesh (human) by the Spirit of God did so through the flesh and blood of a human creature; our Lord came to us by the Spirit through the faithfulness of Mary. Later on in the reconciling mission of God, as Jesus stood on the threshold of his mission to carry out the will of God the Father, the Holy Spirit was there creating space by opening up every aspect of Jesus and his life to embody the will of God perfectly (Luke 2:40-52), engaging fully in God's mission "on earth as in heaven."

In this unfolding story of God's mission, the steadfast love of God continued to reach out to Jesus through the mission of the Spirit, so that in those trying and turning-point days, there was the Spirit, comforting and empowering Jesus to remain faithful in the mission of God. For example, the Spirit of God who descended on Jesus at his baptism (Matt. 3:13-17) was the same Spirit who drove him into the wilderness (4:1-11). Later at Gethsemane, while facing the direst of circumstances, Jesus sweat drops of blood (Luke 22:41-45) and, once again, the Spirit remained unwavering in God's mission by enabling him to stand firm in faithfulness to the will of God. While anguishing in this climactic trial, Jesus prayed the prayer truly born of the Spirit, "Not my will but yours be done" (v. 42). Mary once had prayed this prayer, "Let it be with me according to your word" (1:38). And it is conceivable to imagine that as Jesus "grew in stature and wisdom" (Luke 2:40), Mary taught Jesus how to pray that same prayer of willful surrender. Jesus taught the heart of that prayer to all his disciples in the patterned prayer we know most familiarly as the Lord's Prayer, "Your kingdom come. Your will be done, on earth as it is in heaven" (Matt. 6:10).

Finally, in the gospel mission of condescending love, the Spirit was always there breathing into (inspiring in) Jesus the *ways* of God's reconciling mission, and in the same breath the Spirit was always there breathing with (conspiring) Jesus to complete God's reconciling mission through all the *ways* of the cross and the resurrection. By the abiding presence of the Spirit, Jesus was able to be authentically human and face God in the same way the whole human family faces God, that is, in complete trust. By the constant indwelling presence of the Spirit, our Lord was able to face God as we all must, and learn obedience—dependence and trust in the mission of the Spirit—through the things he suffered (Heb. 5:8-9). Moreover, it was only by the Spirit that Christ could face the darkness of the cross in the hope of resurrection, and it was finally in the power of the resurrection that Christ was able to "trample down death by death."[1] In other words, it was through the faithfulness of the Spirit that Jesus was able to live after the *missio Dei,* fulfill the will of his Father, and become "the pioneer of [our] salvation" (Heb. 2:10). The mission of Christ was fulfilled in the mission of "the Spirit . . . who raised [him] from the dead" (Rom. 8:11).

THE MISSION OF THE HOLY SPIRIT AT PENTECOST

"Wherever the Holy Spirit is, there is the Church of Christ," said Irenaeus, reflecting that wherever the Spirit is, there is the Son, and wherever the Son is, there is the Spirit, breathing the life, energy, and love of God on all flesh. Consequently, as Christ would bear the Spirit in the Incarnation, the mission of Christ already was bearing witness to the future of the new day of Pentecost in God's mission of reconciling love. This was made plain when our Lord promised the outpouring of the Holy Spirit to continue his mission and fulfill the will of the Father long after his ascension. In faithfulness to the incarnate mission of Christ, the mission of the Spirit would bring to completion at Pentecost the mission of Christ in the Incarnation, by constituting a new kind of embodied *koinōnia* in the ongoing mission of our risen Lord "on earth as it is in heaven."

The mission of the Holy Spirit is the mission of the church. In faithfulness to the reconciling mission of God, the mission of the Spirit at Pentecost gathers up the "dismembered" people of God and "re-members" or reconnects them into the body of Christ. The Spirit gathers the church into the fellowship of the triune God, then sends (breathes out) the church into the world to be bearers of God's reconciling mission. Constituted by the Spirit, the mission of the *gathered* and *sent* church is the mission of the Holy Spirit.

TWO OLD TESTAMENT STORIES EVOKING PENTECOST

Since Pentecost was a radically new day in history, the birthday of the church, we must ask, What is the mission of the Holy Spirit in the church of Christ? What is the mission of the people of God who have been reconstituted into a new kind of fellowship in the ongoing mission of our risen Lord? How should we understand the signs of Pentecost within the grand narrative(s) of God's mission? Do some of the previous stories of God's mission already "participate" in the promise and hope of Pentecost? We note two, the story of the Tower of Babel (Gen. 11:1-9) and Ezekiel's vision of the valley of dry bones (Ezek. 37:1-14). These stories anticipate in their warning and promise of what life in the Spirit is meant to be and will be. These stories illuminate God's promised mission of the Holy Spirit to pour out on all flesh the gift of pentecostal fellowship in the body of Christ.

The Tower of Babel

Crucial to understanding the story of the Tower of Babel is God's earlier blessing of Noah and his sons after the flood, including God's command to "be fruitful and multiply, and fill the earth" (Gen. 9:1). Instead of filling the earth, Noah's immediate descendants attempted to build a city and a tower to the heavens. Full of hubris, they chose to defy God's blessings and commands, attempting instead to insulate themselves with the benefit of a common language. Their defiant attempt to construct a life of freedom from God and the rest of the earth ended in division and alienation. Cut off from one another, they became babblers in their isolation.

This story could be torn from the pages of Genesis and reprinted with hardly a revision to portray life today. Much of our experience seems to echo the same idolatrous isolation and fragmented divisions, from one another and from God, as was sketched from the characters of this account. Our broken relationships share a similar story with similar patterns of babbling confusion. This ancient story already teaches that our lives ultimately are connected to one another only as blessed by God's life-giving Spirit.

Lives lived in gratitude and deeply connected to one another are a sign of breathing deeply of the Spirit of God. Alternatively, if we live our lives in defiance of God and God's blessings, life is marked by ingratitude, which only deepens the rift until we are cut off from the rest of our human family. An ungrateful life chokes off life and breath, until, in the end, we die to all our relationships: we die in relation to God, to the human family, and to the rest of the physical creation. Cut off from one another and living in ingratitude, we "babble" in all our relationships until there is no breath left in us and we die.

Ezekiel's Valley of Dry Bones

We turn to Ezekiel's vision of the valley of dry bones (Ezek. 37:1-14). Ezekiel sat in the middle of the valley floor and surveyed a wide vista, littered with the dried-up, sun-bleached, and dismembered skeletons that comprised the "whole house of Israel." That these were the dead bones of Israel's house is confirmed later in the vision when God described them as crying out, "Our bones are dried up, and our hope is lost; we are cut off completely" (v. 11). Now let us listen with hopeful imagination, as God asked Ezekiel, "Mortal, can these bones live?" (v. 3). Hear what God said through Ezekiel to all those disconnected and dried-up bones, "I will cause breath to enter you, and you shall live. I will lay sinews on you, and will cause flesh to come upon you, and cover you with skin, and put breath in you, and you shall live; and you shall know that I am the Lord" (vv. 5-6).

What would happen next in the story is enough to take our breath away. As Ezekiel prophesied according to the promise of God, a wind began to stir in the valley and Ezekiel heard the strangest of sounds, unlike any he had heard before. In the fierce stirring of the wind all the dried-up and detached bones were raised up from the dust of the earth. In that stirring wind came the terrific rattling and clanging together of all those dismembered skeletons. As the Spirit/Wind blew, the Spirit began to "reconnect" and "reassemble" the "whole house of Israel." Dried-up and disconnected bones were reconnected, with tendons, ligaments, and muscle, and covered with skin as God had promised (vv. 7-8).

But God was not yet finished. "There was no breath in them" (v. 8) as God had promised there would be (v. 6). Despite the Spirit's re-membering of those disconnected bones in the dismembered body of Israel, the reassembled bones did not yet live! How can the body live without the breath of God? So God continued to speak to and through Ezekiel. "Prophesy to the breath, prophesy, mortal, and say to the breath: Thus says the Lord God: Come from the four winds, O breath, and breathe upon these slain, that they may live" (v. 9).

If the prior scene of the re-membering and the reconnecting of the "whole house of Israel" were enough to take *our* breath away, the last scene in Ezekiel's vision (v. 10) gives it back. As commanded by God, Ezekiel spoke God's word, the breath came into them, and they lived! A vast multitude of formerly dried-up, dead, and detached bones stood up on their feet, completely reconnected, fully clothed, and alive with the breath of God! So there should be no more dismembering of Israel's house, God promised through Ezekiel to renew Israel's hope once again: "I am going to open your graves, and bring you up from your graves, O my people; and I will bring you back to the land of Israel. . . . I will put my spirit within you, and you shall live, and I will place you on your own soil; then you shall know that I, the Lord, have spoken and will act, says the Lord" (vv. 12, 14).

Ezekiel's vision is a vision of the Spirit *poured out on all flesh.* It is a vision to open our eyes and stir our hearts with healing imagination. It is a vision of promise and hope for renewal. On many levels Ezekiel's vision of the Spirit is a vision that anticipates and participates in Pentecost with its crucial question, "Mortal, can these bones live?"

THE DAY OF PENTECOST AND BEYOND

Looking backward through the prism of these two stories, we can see more clearly in the story of the day of Pentecost what our Lord has done for us and our salvation in the reconciling mission of God. Once again, when the sound of a mighty rushing wind filled the house, tongues like flames of fire fell on Jesus' disciples assembled in the upper room. A tongue of fire rested on each of them, and they began to speak in many languages (Acts 2:1-4). When the Spirit came on the day of Pentecost, God's judgment on the Tower of Babel was reversed.

In Babel its inhabitants had used their language to separate and disconnect from the rest of the human family. In Jerusalem at Pentecost, the Spirit reversed that pattern of "dismembering" and gave the gift of languages as a means of "re-membering" within the body of Christ. By the gift of languages, the family of God was *sent* to network and reconnect with the rest of the human family in the reconciling mission of God. No longer would the people of God be cut off and divided from God and one another, whether by language, by race, by culture, by story and history, or by geography. Instead of isolation, the Holy Spirit's gift of pentecostal fellowship made possible unimpeded access to God and to one another.

When the Spirit came on the day of Pentecost, all who had been called out from the corners of the globe (from the perspective of Jerusalem) and instructed to wait for the Spirit's outpouring, the Spirit gathered up, *"re-membered,"* and *reconnected.* The Spirit reconstituted them into a new body of pentecostal fellowship, the body of Christ. On the day of Pentecost the mission of the Spirit gathered and reconstituted the people of God into the *koinōnia* of the triune God. Through the Spirit they could partake of God's life and dwell in God as God dwells in us (2 Pet. 1:4). By virtue of the Spirit's gathering, this partaking of God's life (fellowship) includes participating in the fellowship of God's mission.

As we are gathered up into the fellowship of triune love, the Spirit heals our babbling divisions, our loss of memory and identity, by *re-membering* us into the body of Christ, and *sending* us back into the world to be a sacrament of holy, healing, and enabling love for the life of the whole world. In the mission of the Spirit, the people of God have been *gathered* into fellowship with God and *re-membered* into the body of Christ to live after the heart and mission of God. This is the mission of the Holy Spirit, the Spirit of our crucified and risen Lord!

A Prayer of and for the Church Today

Continue to breathe in (*inspire*) your church, O Holy Spirit, breath of God. Continue to breathe with (*conspire*) your church so your church may "re-member" and be "re-membered," that we may breathe back, with all *our* breath, your praise and thanksgiving.

Glory to the Father, and to the Son and to the Holy Spirit;
As it was in the beginning, is now, and will be forever.
                                                              Amen.

10
THE CHURCH EXISTS BY MISSION
K. Steve McCormick

In anticipation of the Church of the Nazarene's centennial celebration (2008), the Board of General Superintendents crafted a new mission statement. The mission of the denomination is "to make Christlike disciples in the nations." This statement is designed to reflect a global mission for a global church. Perhaps nothing captures the heart and spirit of this renewed vision of a global mission more than the words of Emil Brunner, "The Church exists by mission as fire exists by burning."[1]

IT TAKES A CHURCH

From the Great Commission of Christ to the Spirit's new day of Pentecost, the message is clear: it takes a church "to make Christlike disciples in the nations." The church cannot *be* the church apart from *mission.* The people of God cannot live out of the *missio Dei* apart from Christ and his church.

A little over forty-five years ago, Albert Outler asked his fellow Methodists, "Do Methodists have a doctrine of the Church?"[2] Now as the Church of the Nazarene embarks on a second century of global mission, this missional urgency and crossroads in its history make it theologically necessary to ask, Do Nazarenes have a doctrine of the church? On the surface, the answer to that question for both the Methodist and the Nazarene traditions is the deceptively simple response, "Yes, of course we do."[3] Yet when Nazarenes probe into the rationale for their practice(s) of mission, it is not always clear that a coherent and robust doctrine of the church directly sustains the mission "to make Christlike disciples in the nations."

In the earliest days of Nazarene mission, the founders see' comfortable as a movement for mission rather than being an establisن... church *with* a mission. Often in the early stages of numerous Christian movements, the nature of mission has been described in strongly anti-institutional tones. Expressed sentiments often have reflected suspicions about becoming an established body for fear that such a posture would smother the fire of God's mission. Thus the strong call to mission frequently eclipsed a clear sense of what it meant to be the church?[4]

Historically in revivalist movements, the zeal to evangelize the world through the power of the gospel has been motivated and guided almost exclusively by a deeply personal experience of salvation. The personal, transformative power of the gospel has shaped the sense of mission. It has inspired people to preach the good news throughout the world. The gospel can be an intensely personal experience—an experience of Christ *for me,* that seems to be *immediate* and *direct,* frequently compelling one to witness about God's grace. Such experiences, however, sometimes neglect the necessity of the church (the body of Christ) as the embodiment and mediator of that grace. An experience-driven tradition and a burning desire to spread this good news has made it seem, at times, as though Christ's church is secondary to his Great Commission (Matt. 28:19-20).

— central to mission (χ just indiv. effort)

FOR THE LIFE OF THE WORLD

Once this inexpressible joy of salvation is fixed firmly to a fervent missional pragmatism with a strong bias for an anti-institutional "church," it often overlooks the full warrant of scriptural witness that testifies to *how* and *why* the church is to be a sacrament of God's reconciling mission "for the life of the world."[5] The members of Christ's body, his disciples, now exist to offer the new and unending life of Christ by *living in the way of the Cross* through the power of the resurrection. They give their very lives in the same self-giving, self-emptying way of Christ. Unfortunately, private and individualistic renderings of salvation have tended to read the Great Commission of Christ as persistently overshadowing the new day of Pentecost and the Spirit's "new reorienting way"[6] for how we are called to live out of God's mission as members of Christ's body. Consequently, even the most sincere desire to heed Christ's command to go into all the world and make disciples of all nations, baptizing them in the name of the Father and of the Son and of the Holy Spirit, and teaching them to obey everything that Christ has commanded us, will not always make the necessary connection that such a command to mission is synonymous with *being* the church.

Christ's church exists in mission by the power of the Spirit through all the "gathered" and "connected" members of Christ's body. "Wherever the Spirit is, there is the Church of Christ," said the early church writer, Irenaeus. God Almighty, who made heaven and earth, has come to us in Christ, pouring out his Spirit on all creation, gathering and connecting the people of God from all the nations into the fellowship (*koinōnia*) of God's mission. For Irenaeus, Christ and the Spirit were "the two hands of God" that keep gathering and connecting the members of Christ's body into the mission of the church because God is by nature missional. God is a missionary God who is forever *sending God's love*—that is, God's very self (Emmanuel)—to gather and connect the whole world into the fellowship of God. Out of the abundance of God's unending love for the world, God sent God's Son to reconcile all of creation by the transforming energy of God's Spirit through the power of the cross and the resurrection. This triune God who is in name and nature love[7] is a missionary God. God is steadfastly drawing the people of God in all the nations of the world into the body of Christ to bear witness to the gospel and to be a sacrament of God's reconciling mission "for the life of the world."[8]

INSTITUTED BY CHRIST, CONSTITUTED BY THE SPIRIT

When the gospel story is told in strong missional language, it must be explained that without Christ and the Spirit there can be no church. Likewise, apart from the mission of Christ and the Spirit there can be no mission of the church. To think of Christ's disciples as carrying out the mission of Christ apart from the mission of the church would be to contradict the very nature of Christ and the Spirit. The way God was in Christ reconciling the world by the Spirit is continued in the way Christ *institutes* and the Spirit *constitutes* the church to "become participants of the divine nature" (2 Pet. 1:4)* by participating in the reconciling mission of God (2 Cor. 5:11-21).

If we follow the narrative of Scripture and hold fast to the connections that Christ and the Spirit embody in the *koinōnia* of God's mission, then we must return to where Christian identity and discipleship is formed, that is, to our baptism. We have been buried and raised to new life in Christ. Sealed by baptism and marked as Christ's disciples, we must allow Jesus' probing question, "Who do you say that I am?" (Matt. 16:15), and our own baptismal response, to define and pattern the kind of embodied participation in the *missio Dei* that is the true mark of Christian discipleship.

The *way* of Christian discipleship in the body of Christ is the *way* of God's reconciling mission. Today the church is in urgent need of the Spirit's rekindling for mission. In the spirit of Christian discipleship, all Christ's disciples must listen attentively to Christ as he asks the church, "Who do you say that I am?" Only by the illumining power of the Spirit can the church discern in prayer the faithful response to Jesus' inquiry that confesses Jesus as Lord! Such a confession is the mark of Christian discipleship—a discipleship that comes only by the Spirit who enables Christ's disciples to hear and respond to Christ's call to participate in the *koinōnia* (fellowship) of God's reconciling mission. As all the people of God, praying and listening obediently with burning hearts and inquiring minds, we are called as Christ's disciples to partake of God's very nature by participating in the reconciling mission of God.

As Christ's disciples, why then do we often assume we can make disciples in the nations without Christ's body, the church? Is it possible we have failed to understand the nature of our baptism, not only in relation to Christ but in relation to the church? Would it not follow that we have failed to understand our calling to make disciples in the nations by baptizing them in the name of the Father, Son, and Holy Spirit and teaching (*catechesis*) them in the *way* of salvation, with the knowledge of and obedience (*ascesis*) to Christ's words, deeds, and destiny? What is the connection between baptism and the church? What is the correlation of our baptism into the triune God and Christian discipleship? Despite the

---

*All Scripture quotations in this chapter are from the NRSV, except as noted.

church's best intentions, we must ask ourselves, why do we persist in splitting the church's *mission* from the church's *being?*

THE GREAT COMMISSION AND PENTECOST

As penetrating and integrated as these questions are, we cannot tackle them one by one or even collectively in this short essay. Taken as a whole, however, they do serve to pinpoint a more serious problem that continues to plague the church and those called to make disciples in the nations. Our repeated failure to connect the *being* of the church with the *mission* of the church is a failure to envision Pentecost as an extended fulfillment of the Incarnation. It is a failure to read the Great Commission as a promise to be embodied and lived out through the fulfillment of Pentecost. The command of the Great Commission hangs on the promise of Pentecost. Who Jesus is and who we are as his disciples, following in his *way* of making disciples, cannot be fully grasped and embodied apart from the new day in history that was key to making "all things new" (Rev. 21:5), that is, the day of Pentecost.

Before the day of Pentecost, there was the way of the cross. In the cross we find the way that God in Christ by the Spirit met us, dwelt with and in us, reconciled us, loved us and continues to love us. Consider how the gospel of John narrates the passion of Christ as making a *new way*. When Jesus knew that all now was finished on the cross, he said: "I am thirsty" (19:28) to fulfill the scripture. In that moment, in the words of Martin Smith, "All of God thirst for all of humankind and all of humankind thirst for all of God."[9] In the next moment, after the sponge was touched to his lips, Jesus cried, "It is finished" (v. 30). He bowed his head and gave up his spirit. In that finished moment, Christ exhaled, breathed out, released the Spirit. Our Lord died! In that finished moment, when Christ was crucified, his Spirit was breathed out on all creation.

Mark's gospel tells us, "The curtain of the temple was torn in two, from top to bottom" (Mark 15:38). Matthew's gospel adds, "The earth shook, and the rocks were split. The tombs also were opened, and many bodies of the saints who had fallen asleep were raised" (Matt. 27:51-52). In that finished moment of reconciliation when all creation received the Spirit, something radically new happened. In Christ, God had cleared the obstacles away. We have unimpeded access to God! In that finished moment, the cross of Christ opened up heaven on earth and pierced holes of glory into all our darkness, making way for Pentecost.

Pentecost, that radically new day in history that made "all things new," was the result of the Father having *sent* the Son and the Spirit[10] to accomplish the *missio Dei* of the cross and resurrection on earth, in time and history. The descent of the Spirit on that unique day constituted Christ and his church, and opened space in the *oikodomē* (the church figured as a building) for all the gathered to participate in the life and reconciling mission of the triune God on earth. Not only was the day of Pentecost a new way for the people of God in history, but it also was a new way for the triune God in history. Simply put, for the first time in history, through the work of Christ and the Spirit, a new window into the house of God was opened to all of creation. In this new, reorienting way the gathered people of God have unfettered access to their God, and God has unhindered access to them.

Moreover, as the Spirit connects God to us and us to God, the people of God will have new access to one another. In the fellowship of God's mission, complete strangers who once were divided by language, culture, race, geography, and life experiences can be brought together as brothers and sisters in a new family. Christ's disciples are connected in a new kinship in a new way and, embodied together, can discover new ways of making disciples in the nations and enlarging the family of God.

This means the Spirit metaphorically connects the nerves and sinews of Christ's body by gathering and connecting the people of God into the *koinōnia* of God's reconciling mission. In this renewed fellowship, not only does God belong to us in a new way, but we now, likewise, belong to God and to one another in this new way.

OUR MISSIONAL CHALLENGE

This kind of *real* belonging in the fellowship of God's reconciling mission is more than a gregarious, clublike fellowship. It is a new way of being that reflects the very nature of God and God's mission. Pentecostal fellowship is the new way of "making Christlike disciples in the nations."

With hearts set ablaze by the contagious fire of fellowship (*koinōnia*), let us partake of God's very nature by participating in the *missio Dei*.

As the church embarks on a new century of global mission, let us listen obediently to Christ as he asks his disciples, "Who do you say that I am?" This is the place where we will hear the Spirit of Christ call the church to bear witness to the gospel and be a sacrament of God's reconciling mission. Rekindled by the Spirit's fire of missional urgency, we can and *must* move forward with a coherent and vigorous doctrine of the church that informs and sustains the fellowship of God's reconciling mission.

11

THE ALREADY/NOT YET KINGDOM OF GOD

Ron Benefiel

Jesus came proclaiming the kingdom of God. He taught in parables of the kingdom, performed miracles that were signs of the kingdom, and lived a life that embodied and illustrated the kingdom. Everything was subject to his authority. The wind and the waves obeyed his command. People bound by sin were set free. Evil spirits were cast out. The sick were healed, the lame were raised up and walked. Sight was restored to the blind. Even the dead were resurrected! And Jesus' message to his disciples was that we are to seek first the kingdom (Matt. 6:33).

The kingdom of God is the rule or reign of God. Whatever or whoever is subject to his authority is under the authority of the kingdom. We do not "build" the kingdom of God. Rather, God invites us to enter (18:3; 19:23), receive (Mark 10:15), or inherit (Matt. 25:34) the kingdom. When we enter the kingdom, we also participate with what God is doing in the world (10:7-8). The mission of the kingdom is always God's mission. Our calling in the church is to bear witness to what God is doing in the world, primarily by proclaiming and exhibiting the character of the kingdom in the grace-filled stories of redemption in our lives, in the nature of our relationships together, and in the way we engage the world around us.

Our confident hope as Christians is that Jesus is coming back to earth to establish his kingdom fully and forever. When he returns, the dead in Christ will be resurrected. Faithful saints from every language and every tribe will welcome his return and will be gathered together as one people, reconciled to God and one another, kneeling before him in worship, wonder, and praise. In that day, there will be no sorrow, no sickness, no suffering, no death. As God created the universe in the beginning, the new creation will reflect its original pristine beauty and purity. We will forever be with the Lord.

But what about these days? These days in which we remember the stories of Jesus and look forward to his return? What about these days in between Jesus' ascension into heaven and his return in the final day? What is God doing in the world these days? Days that seem to be characterized by discord and disunity. Days when most people are not healed and the dead are not resurrected. Days when even the creation itself seems to teeter on the verge of coming undone. How are we to think and act and live as followers of Jesus who remember the stories of Jesus' presence and power, who look forward to his return, but who live in a fallen, broken, sinful world?

SIGNS OF THE ALREADY/NOT YET KINGDOM

Thanks be to God that in these times "in between" Jesus' ascension into heaven and his soon return, we have not been abandoned or left on our own (John 14:18). The Father has sent the Spirit in power (Acts 2) to be with us and to lead and teach us (John 14:26). Even when we get discouraged, or are faced with a real-life tragedy, or when it looks like the forces of evil are winning, the grace and power of God are at work around us. We see these signs of the kingdom in our world when people's lives are transformed by the grace of God. We see these signs when people who have been alienated from each other, or at war with one another, are reconciled not only to God but also to one another (Eph. 2:11-22). We see signs of the kingdom when people are miraculously healed. We also see these signs when, by the power of the Spirit, the church lives up to its calling of being a holy, merciful, just, hospitable, and loving community.

Some scholars call this in-between time the "already/not yet" kingdom of God. By that, they mean the kingdom is here "already" as the power of God in Christ Jesus through the Spirit at work all around us, but it is also "not yet," in that it will only be when Jesus returns that the kingdom will be established fully and forever. The "already" means that the kingdom that will be fully realized when Jesus returns is partially realized now. The work of God we see in our world today is only a glimpse or a foretaste of what we will see when Jesus returns. But even now, by the power of God, the kingdom proclaimed, embodied, and promised by Jesus comes to us (Mark 9:1; Luke 11:20) or is "breaking in" to our world in these in-between days. The end (the kingdom in the final day) also is breaking in to the here and now. When we see God at work as the kingdom "breaks in" on us, it renews our hope in anticipation of Jesus' return, when everything will be made new according to his will and purpose.

FORGIVENESS AND RECONCILIATION

In 1994, tribal violence broke out in Rwanda between the Hutus and the Tutsis. In one of the most horrific events of the twentieth century, approximately 800,000 men, women, and children were murdered in the span of about three months. Tensions between the two tribal groups persist even today. Nazarene leaders in Rwanda were a great example of peace and reconciliation following the genocide, bringing people together and even forming a choir of Hutus and Tutsis that traveled around the country singing together as a witness to the reconciling power of God. In 1999, church leaders sponsored a reconciliation conference, asking a number of people to tell their experiences related to the conflict and the story of how God had brought peace and healing to their churches, their villages, and their families. One young follower of Jesus told this story:

My name is Frederick. I am twenty-three years old. Genocide happened when I was a lad. Even though I belong to the tribe whose people participated in murdering their fellow human beings, I did not participate in it. In 1998 there were mass killings of people done by the malicious killers. This time the target group was the Hutus whom they thought and believed were loyal to the Tutsis. We were in a public commuter mini-bus. It was stopped. They ordered all the people to get out of the bus. They pushed us into a nearby bush where they murdered all the Tutsis who were with us. They cut off my two hands, accusing me of being a servant of the Tutsis. It took me eight hours before I was taken to the hospital naked. I had lost a lot of blood. But by the grace of the Lord I survived. I was treated, but the fact still remains that I can do nothing with my hands. I kept on wondering if God can forgive the enemies who cut off my two hands. What had I done to deserve this punishment? Later on after great consideration of the power of God who spared my life at the time when my hands were being cut off, I decided with the help of the Holy Spirit to forgive those who made me a disabled person. At this moment I am ruled by the grace of God, and I thank him for calling me to be the servant he anointed to preach the message of hope and forgiveness. I can do everything through Christ who gives me strength.[1]

Frederick's forgiveness of his enemies goes contrary to every natural urge most of us have for retribution. His testimony speaks of something that transcends human instinct. In the middle of the Rwandan genocide, with all its horror and death, is this sign of the kingdom, an act of forgiveness that defies human reason. Of course, there were many others, too, people of God responding in obedience to God's call for peace, forgiveness, and reconciliation. It reminds us of the voice of Jesus saying, "You have heard that it was said, 'You shall love your neighbor and hate your enemy.' But I say to you, Love your enemies and pray for those who persecute you" (Matt. 5:43-44, NRSV).

Frederick's story renews our hope for the fulfillment of the kingdom in the final day. For in that day, all the people of God will be reconciled not only to God but also to one another. There will be no more war, no tribal conflicts, no killing, maiming, grief, or pain. Meanwhile, the kingdom of peace and righteousness (Rom. 14:17) is breaking in on us here and now by the power of the Spirit, right in the middle of our pain-filled world!

RENEWAL

I'm a backpacker. For thirty-five years, I have spent at least a week almost every summer hiking with friends through the majesty of the backcountry of Yosemite National Park. Frequently, I have found it to be a place of retreat and renewal as I have followed the trails through the mountain wilderness, listened to stories around the campfire, chased off squirrels and bears, and wandered off on my own to meet with God.

I remember one trip, in particular, feeling especially tired and worn out as I headed into the mountains. I probably was close to burnout from my work in ministry and was in desperate need of a word of hope or encouragement from God. The second or third day, I wandered off by myself over to Emeric Lake. I sat down near the shore, opened my pocket

Bible to Psalm 42 and began to read aloud, "As the deer pants for the water brooks, so pants my soul for You, O God" (v. 1, NKJV). As I began to sing the words of the psalm, the sky turned dark and I could see in the distance the clouds overflowing, with streaks of rain falling on rocks and trees below.

I continued to sing, longing to know once again the intimacy and vitality of the presence of God in my soul. I watched as the rain came closer and began to form gentle ripples in the mirrored stillness at the far end of the lake. I watched as the pattern of raindrops on the water slowly came closer and closer. Then the rain began to fall on me! In that moment, the water drops from the sky were like drops of grace falling from heaven. It was as though the Spirit of the Lord was being poured out on my soul, soaking me in the intimate presence and power of God! I knew in the deepest part of my being that I was known and loved by God.

For me in that moment, the grace of God freely flowed like a river into my spiritual wilderness. It was a sign of the kingdom for me, the kingdom of God breaking into my world, revealing again who God is and what God is doing, in *me*! In this time in-between, it was a reminder that the kingdom has come in Christ Jesus and is here among us through the presence of the Spirit. It was a word of hope, a moment of transfiguration by a mountain lake, in which I experienced a glimpse of what it will be like to be forever in the presence of God when Jesus comes back again.

LOVE, MERCY, JUSTICE, HOPE

As people of the kingdom, participating in the mission of God in the world, we take seriously God's loving concern for those who are broken, lost, and suffering. With him and in him, we share in Jesus' poured-out, incarnational, redemptive love for the world. Inevitably, we find ourselves drawn to the poor, to those in need at the margins of society, always pointing people to Jesus with a cup of cold water, a warm blanket, a listening ear, a helping hand. The amazing thing is that sometimes—quite often, actually—we see the kingdom "break in" right in front of our eyes as the hopeless become hopeful, the weary find strength, the lost are found, sinners are saved, and relationships are reconciled. Signs of the kingdom!

As people of the kingdom, we are a people of hope, looking forward to the great and glorious day of Christ's return (Phil. 3:20-21). We begin to realize we have a stake not only in this world, as we participate in God's mission of redemptive love, but also in the world to come, as we eagerly await that day. Focusing our attention on Jesus, looking forward to his return, we find we are changed—John says we "purify" ourselves (1 John 3:3). We are, of course, continually and repeatedly sustained in our participation in God's mission by the presence and power of God through the Spirit. But we also are sustained and changed by God's grace as we look forward to—"live into"—the coming kingdom. And with Christians of all the ages we pray, "Thy kingdom come."

As we focus our attention on Jesus and the already/not yet kingdom, we begin to understand our calling to be witnesses of Christ and of that kingdom. The people of God are to proclaim the kingdom (Luke 9:60), to bear witness to the kingdom by being a living example (or at least a foreshadowing) of what the kingdom looks like. When relationships are restored and the whole body of Christ comes together with no distinction between "Jew or Greek, . . . slave or free, . . . male and female" (Gal. 3:27-28, NRSV), or when we who have lived sinfully in rebellion against God repent of our sins and become disciples of Jesus, we become signs of the kingdom. When we who have been made new in Christ care for the poor and visit those who are sick or in prison, we witness to the mercy and justice of God and the nature of the kingdom (Matt. 25:31-46). We are illustrations of the kingdom as the redemptive work of God transforms us both personally and corporately into a people who reflect the holy character of God.

HEALING

For fourteen years, I had the privilege of serving as pastor of First Church of the Nazarene in Los Angeles. The church was especially active in ministering to and among the poor in the urban core. There were so many needs and so few resources, it seemed we always were on the edge. At one point, over the course of several months, we had an especially difficult time as a number of key leaders moved away and three key lay leaders died. I wondered how we could sustain such losses and carry on the ministry we believed God had called us to. In the middle of this time of grief and loss, God performed a miracle named "Spencer." Spencer's mother, Julie, wrote the following account:

> In the fourth month of my first pregnancy, my doctor detected an irregular heartbeat in our baby and immediately referred us to a specialist. After agreeing to have an amniocentesis done we waited for a couple of weeks to find out the results. When we went back, the doctor gave us the good news that the baby was a boy! He then gave us the grim news that our baby's heart was not fully developed and that he would probably not live through the full term of the pregnancy and certainly would not survive the delivery. The doctor then explained that there was some genetic defect indicated by the review of the baby's DNA. The doctor wanted to do an ultrasound to take one more look at the baby's heart. While looking at the monitor he again reiterated how sorry he was and he reassured me that I was young and could have more children. Leaving the office that day I could hardly see to sign out as tears filled my eyes. Royce and I hardly spoke as we drove back to our apartment. The first phone call we made when we got back home was to our pastor, Ron, who came right over. Ron tried to comfort us as best he could in that situation and promised to call the church to prayer. During those last months of my pregnancy I wavered between holding out hope that God would heal this baby and just letting my hopes for this child go. During this time of uncertainty in my life, the hymn "It Is Well with My Soul" came to mean so much to me. My faith was truly strengthened as I knew that no matter how this turned out, God and my church family would be there for me and I would somehow make it through. The wonderful ending to this story is that our son, Spencer, was born healthy and after several tests on his heart the doctors could not find anything wrong! More important is the impact his healing had on our church. When Spencer was just a couple of weeks old, we took him to the teens' Wednesday service and Jeff Carr, the youth leader, held Spencer in his arms as he told those kids that they could never say they had not seen a miracle because those kids and others had prayed for this baby and

now Spencer was there as proof that God is still active in our lives. About seven boys put their money together, bought Spencer a pair of baby Michael Jordan basketball shoes, and presented them to us that night. Spencer became the youth group mascot.[2]

Spencer was living proof, a sign from heaven, that God had not forgotten us. In the middle of our discouragement, God showed his love for us in the form of a little boy. In the middle of our grief, here was the miracle birth of a baby, a symbol of life and hope. This miracle was not only for Spencer and his parents but also for our whole community. In the wake of death, Spencer's miraculous, healthy birth became a sign: the already/not yet kingdom of God had broken in on us!

A FINAL WORD

The kingdom of God has come in Christ Jesus and will be fully established when Jesus returns. Even now, God in Christ Jesus by the Spirit is at work in our world. The kingdom is breaking in on us. The end of the story is breaking into the middle. There are signs of the kingdom in reconciliation, in healing, and in redemption all around us. We are called to be witnesses of this already/not yet kingdom. As we are transformed by the Spirit of God into the holy people of God, we "live into the kingdom," becoming what God intends for us to be, a glimpse, a living illustration, of what the kingdom will look like when Jesus returns. As servants in his kingdom, we eagerly look forward to the return of our King. Come quickly, Lord Jesus!

12

WHAT IS THE POINT OF GOD'S MISSION?

Brent D. Peterson

I have always been good at math. I am a very concrete thinker and numbers made sense to me at an early age. However, this passion and zeal for numbers came at the expense of any artistic talent. In second grade I loved Tuesdays, but hated Wednesdays. Tuesdays were math days and my teacher allowed me to work ahead at my own blistering pace. The glory of excelling on Tuesday was met by the doldrums of mediocrity on Wednesday. Wednesday was painting day. While Tuesdays boosted my fragile ego by my success in solving math problems, every Wednesday I would paint the same tree—brown trunk, with a green bush at the top of it, and one flower in a field of grass, with a sun in the upper left corner.

I was always confused about the purpose of art. I was trying to paint something, but what was my painting seeking to do? What was it accomplishing? Math had a purpose. It involved counting money, telling time, and finding out, if my dad was on a train going from Indianapolis to Denver that left at 1 P.M. Central Time going sixty miles per hour, at what time I would have to leave and at what rate of speed I would have to go if I were on a train in Seattle heading to Denver and wanted to beat him. This was important stuff! In figuring out these "real-life problems" I must confess that finding concrete answers provided a certain sense of power.

My love and passion for math continued into high school until my senior year. In my senior year I met my match, calculus. Until calculus, I could grasp the point of what I was doing. I will never forget how I could get the right answers, but my tiny brain did not grasp what the answers meant and how that information could be useful. Because of my limited brain capacity, math had become art. It was pointless—or was it?

This larger conversation concerns the mission of God and the role Christians play in God's work in the world. But what is the point of God's mission? What is the final end? Such a question has the danger of becoming a math problem (calculus excluded). If you had asked me this question when I was a second grader, I could have answered this question just as simply as my second grade math problems. "Sin is the problem and everybody is going to hell. Jesus came to offer forgiveness so I would not go to hell but to heaven." Answering this question was like simple math, no art was needed. I imagine many Christians today might answer in a similar way. The goal of God's mission is that Christians escape hell by going to heaven. As a second grader living in the United States, I imagined heaven, the escape from hell, as a sort of utopian version of Disney Land meets Willy Wonka's Chocolate Factory in Jamaica. While I do fully embrace the promise of heaven, I wonder if God's healing and mission seeks something broader than simply my escaping hell and getting into a place where I get to satisfy all my desires, or at least eat lots of chocolate.

So in this brief essay I am going to consider the main "point" of God's mission by: *first,* exploring how God's mission begins within the church as the body of Christ; *second,* suggesting that God invites Christians, who are being healed, to go into the world God created as sacred, to proclaim and offer the healing and hope of God to those who are lost and in despair; and *third,* affirming that the world is good because God created it and is working toward its redemption; that is why God uses the church to participate in the healing of the world. In light of these explorations, I will argue that the final end of God's healing and mission in the world is the glorification of God. The main point of God's healing in the world is that God may be all in all. God *will* be all in all, as persons love God and love others as they were created in God's image.

THE MISSION BEGINS WITHIN

God sends the church into the world to participate in the world's redemption. However, before the church participates in God's mission out in the world, the church must recognize that God's healing mission begins within the church, the body of Christ. In the gospel of John, on the night before Jesus was killed, he proclaimed, "I give you a new commandment, that you love one another. Just as I have loved you, you also should love one another. By this everyone will know that you are my disciples, if you have love for one another" (13:34-35).* *LOVE*

The love Christians have for one another is the most powerful evangelical tool of the church. The reverse is also true; one of the biggest hindrances to God's healing in the world is Christians not loving each other well. If the body of Christ is full of infighting, jealousy, and discord, the church's mission in the world will be both dishonest and ineffective. Some Christians adopt an escapist attitude, "I want to love the world, but I am tired of church folk." They neglect to consider that the hope of going out in the world is that those currently on the margins may be brought into the church, hopefully a community of love, hope, and accountability. God's healing in the world centers around love. Christians cannot be cruel to each other, all the while pretending to love the world.

WE ARE HEALED IN ORDER TO LOVE

In the tenth chapter of the gospel of Mark is the account of blind Bartimaeus. According to that narrative, Bartimaeus was not healed simply so his life could become more convenient, safe, and comfortable. Bartimaeus was healed so he could follow Jesus. "Jesus said to him, 'Go; your faith has made you well.' Immediately he regained his sight and followed him on the way" (Mark 10:52). Christians are being healed that they might follow Jesus. When following Jesus, persons recognize the hope of God's mission in the world is that *all* may see, that *all* may find hope and life in loving God, ourselves, and others. Christians are being healed to serve, and in their serving God continues to heal Christians, in love. *Healed to follow*

The church goes out not simply to obey a command, but as an act of worship. As the church encounters the piercing, renewing love of God in the communal worship of Scripture, prayers, offering, and the Eucharist, it is transformed to proclaim hope and forgiveness and to be God's flesh and blood in the world. Christians' participation in this mission, sent from the Eucharist, is their primary means of worshipping God during the week. As the church is sent out by the Spirit, all the church does in

---

*All Scripture quotations in this chapter are from the NRSV.

participating in God's mission is doxological. That is to say, the church's participation in God's mission during the week continues their communal worship that began on the Lord's Day.

Participating in God's mission is always an act of worship and thanks for who God is and what God has done and is doing. A danger lurks that participating in God's mission would supplant or separate the church from its primary purpose, the communal worship of God; conversely, participating in God's mission is a crucial aspect of the church's worship from the Lord's Table. The church participates in God's mission, sent from the communal worship of the Word and Table empowered by the Spirit.

Recognizing that the church still needs God's continual healing to love, the church is sent out into the world as those who are being healed, not as those who already are perfected. A posture of humility and hope guards the church from being arrogant and self-righteous. The Christian's participation in God's mission is also the means by which God continues the healing of sanctification to love. In order to embrace fully the healing life God offers, persons must receive such life as a gift from God. Yet here is the great irony of God's mission in the world. The healing God offers cannot be possessed, owned, or controlled; it can only be received by giving one's life back to God. In other words, the only way to embrace God's healing in your life, the only way to save your life, is to give your life away for the love of the world (Matt. 16:25). Receive by Giving

God sends the church out to into the world to continue the ministry Jesus began. Just as Jesus gave his life for the world, so the church, as the body of Christ, is to be broken and spilled out in love before the world. Furthermore, the church goes out among the world to draw and invite the world to worship God and to become part of the body of Christ. The church is sent out into the world as an embodiment (an "enfleshing") of its calling to be the body of Christ.

THE WORLD IS SACRED

The church's participation in God's mission, as it is sent into the world, celebrates that the world is sacred, created good by God. Often some in the church have difficulty speaking about the goodness of creation in light of all the evil we suffer, often at the hands of others.

This fuels the perception of God's mission mentioned earlier, "The point of God's mission is to get me to heaven because this earth is going to burn." Coupled with this idea is that until Christ returns, the church is the only holy space; everything outside is "secular" and "pagan" and should be avoided, perhaps even feared. This sacred-secular dualism no longer should be considered a Christian posture.

While evil does occur in the world, it is a disease God is healing and redeeming. So God sends the church into the world to participate in God's ongoing healing of creation. Therefore, as Wesleyans, in light of the doctrine of prevenient grace—that God is already at work in all the world—the church is not bringing God to the world. Rather, the church is charged with exposing the light of God already present and allowing God's light to shine more brightly. The world was created good, even though, as described in Romans 8:18-25, the creation also cries out for its redemption. God sends the church into the world that God might restore and redeem the world, which points toward the final goal of God's mission.

God sends the church into the world not as imperialists or colonialists, but to name and display, to peel back the layers of God's offered hope of salvation and restoration. The church comes bearing witness to the gospel of hope. Christians embody this hope by testifying that life is found, not in securing and possessing life, but by not being afraid to die. The church comes in love and peace, to embody God's *shalom*—peace, wholeness, and well-being. Therefore, the church is not afraid of anything or anyone. This does not mean evil activity and pockets of darkness do not exist, but that the church comes in light, to expand the light already present and to call for the darkness to cease.

GOD IS THE FINAL END OF THE HEALING

But what is the point of God's healing, God's missionary work in the world? What is the *telos* (the Greek word meaning goal, aim, or purpose) of God's mission? As I alluded to above, God heals persons so they may love God, love themselves, love other Christians, and love all those in the world by proclaiming God's hope and love to those in despair and darkness. Created in the image of God, persons are sanctified, set apart, to love God and others. The love they have received from God they give

Reflecting

away, that God's healing and love may flourish. This sanctification of persons has but one *telos,* the glorification of God. To glorify is, literally, to have one's image shine and radiate from oneself. As Christians love God, themselves, and others, they participate in God's healing mission in the world; in doing so persons are reflecting (glorifying) God to each other.

Some may imagine the world's healing and redemption is the final *telos,* the main point of God's mission. At first glance this feels right, but with more consideration this can lead to a missional idolatry. While the world may be the focus and context, not even the world's healing and restoration is the final purpose, the *end.* With the apostle Paul, we recognize that the final purpose, the main point of God's mission, is the glorification of God:

> But in fact Christ has been raised from the dead, the first fruits of those who have died. For since death came through a human being, the resurrection of the dead has also come through a human being; for as all die in Adam, so all will be made alive in Christ. But each in his own order: Christ the first fruits, then at his coming those who belong to Christ. Then comes the end, when he hands over the kingdom to God the Father, after he has destroyed every ruler and every authority and power. For he must reign until he has put all his enemies under his feet. The last enemy to be destroyed is death. For "God has put all things in subjection under his feet." But when it says, "All things are put in subjection," it is plain that this does not include the one who put all things in subjection under him. When all things are subjected to him, then the Son himself will also be subjected to the one who put all things in subjection under him, *so that God may be all in all.* (1 Cor. 15:20-28, emphasis mine)

The *telos* of the redemption of creation is that God may be all in all. Paul goes on to describe the purpose of those who will be raised from the dead (1 Cor. 15:29-32). In celebrating the resurrection of the dead, even this great hope has one final goal: that God will be all in all. The world's redemption and restoration (including me) is not the final *telos.* Rather, the world's *telos* is to be taken up into God. As recorded in John 17, Jesus prayed that the world may be taken up into the Father as the Son is in the Father, "As you, Father, are in me and I am in you, may they also be in us, so that the world may believe that you have sent me. The glory that you have given me I have given them, so that they may be one, as we are one, I in them and you in me, that they may become completely one, so that the world may know that you have sent me and have loved them even as you have loved me" (vv. 21-23).

The glorification of God is the final end of God's mission, that the church may be one in God. With that *telos* in mind, the church is called to participate in God's mission in the world.

As I have grown older, I have come to appreciate the gift and beauty of art. Art seems to find its real purpose not in some pragmatic end that I can fully grasp and control, exhausting its mystery. Art opens the world to a new imagination, one that refuses to be controlled and contained. In many ways it is the mystery of art that really opens up life, not basic algebra. Similarly, as the final end of God's mission is life in God for God's glory, there is a beauty in the depths of God, the mysterious Other, who invites all to life.

Such an end in God may seem to some like a divine egoism or a waste. Many may seek something more tangible or material than the glorification of God. "Should not we have the ultimate sanctuary, the MEGA-church of all churches?" "Should not we have a kingdom with the biggest buildings, the nicest Learjets, the best golf courses?" Yet even the vision given to John in Revelation 21:4, of having no more tears and mourning, does not aim solely at a human nirvana. Humans are healed to do what they were created to do, to love God, themselves, and others, to worship the Lamb; in doing so they find life, as God ultimately is glorified (Rev. 5:9-13). The redemption of the world, the point of God's mission, is for the glory of God, that God's love may flourish and God may be all in all!

13

THE *MISSIO DEI* AND CULTURE
Bill Selvidge

A KALEIDOSCOPE OF PEOPLE

Every year on the third weekend of August, Kansas City hosts an Ethnic Enrichment Festival in one of its large parks. Flags of many nations line the path leading to the entrance. Representatives from more than forty nations decorate their booths with colors, flags, and other symbols of their countries and cultures. Aromas both familiar and new entice festival-goers to sample exotic foods. People around the pavilion enjoy ethnic musical performances. Colorfully costumed dancers tell the stories of their countries and of their peoples.

Elsewhere, in hundreds of places throughout the world, people join in ministry teams sent out by churches from every continent. They work side by side with believers they may only just have met. Together they build churches and schools, provide medical assistance, or minister in orphanages. Part of the ministry is experiencing an even greater diversity of custom and cultures.

Among this kaleidoscope of peoples, with their amazing variety of customs and cultures, we find God's mission. From the earliest revealing of God's self and God's mission, the redemption and renewal of God's creation has focused on the peoples of the world. God's intention, that *all* peoples of the world know him, is born of the very nature of God.

PEOPLE AND THEIR CULTURES

Based just on the variety of major languages, the world's nearly seven billion people are divided into more than 13,000 clearly distinguishable groups, speaking more than 6,000 languages. That number becomes uncountable when we consider additional factors such as geography, ancestry, local customs, and religious beliefs and practices.

From the earliest days of humanity, people have been identified by how they see the world and, as a result, how they act in the world. These patterns of seeing and acting are known simply as "culture." The way the world "is," how to survive in it, how to enjoy good health while avoiding calamity, how to live a good life but also make sense of death: all these are wrapped up in "culture." The particular way we are to look at the world and to survive in it are taught to us by parents and guardians, and by others around us, from the moment we are born. We are *enculturated* by the people around us as we grow.

Culture is complex. These ways carefully instilled in us have become such a part of us we seldom even think about them. We may consciously arrange a daily schedule without realizing that scheduling itself is a way a particular culture sees the world. We know *when* mealtimes come, but seldom consciously think about how we're going to get the food from the plate—or leaf or paper wrapper—to our mouths; society already has taught us how that is done. I don't stop to consider whether I'll use chopsticks, knife and fork, or just my hands, for eating. We have been taught these things, and this is *culture*. We don't think about them until we encounter someone, or go somewhere, where things are done differently.

CULTURAL MAPS

Charles Kraft compares culture to a map.[1] A road map sets out the paths most people use to get from one place to another. Similarly, a cultural map may be thought of as how the people of a given society see the world and how they order their daily lives to survive in it. Following our cultural (or mental) map makes the most of our everyday life routines. We don't even have to think about most of our actions.

The people of any society simply follow the cultural map their own history, traditions, and customs have given them. But if they decide to try to go where the map has no road, they run into roadblocks. When someone acts differently than society requires, society will point to the map and strongly indicate that sticking to the laid-out roads is the correct way.

If your society's map says, "knife and fork," you can use chopsticks, but try using them every meal for a week, and see what people say. You can choose to ignore the map and get to the "destination" by a different way, but society will let you know this doesn't follow "the way we do things."

The mission of God is found among all the peoples of the world, each with cultural maps already provided. Jesus too had a cultural map. From his earliest days on this earth, Mary and Joseph, the rabbis, other teachers, even his playmates, taught him the map of his society. As long as he stuck to the map, he was just one of many people in that society. But when he challenged aspects of the map, such as the shabby ways society treated some people, then used God as an excuse, not only did he raise eyebrows, but his society worked overtime at getting him back on the accepted "roads."

THE GOSPEL: AFFIRMING CULTURE

The gospel affirms the rich variety of the peoples of the world and their ways of going about daily life.[2] Though God does not give specific details of or for each culture, culture is a gift of God's grace. Culture gives us the capacity to live as groups of people and to find the ways most likely to take us safely from one day, from one season, to the next. Though "culture" often is a loaded term, full of both positive and negative connotations, most aspects of culture are neither good nor bad; they just *are*. These neutral elements of culture, however, can be used either for good or for evil purposes.

Both the Old and the New Testament illustrate the wide variety of peoples and cultures and the importance of taking note of their ways. The Genesis 24 account of Abraham's servant setting off to find a wife for Isaac is rich with descriptions of cultural customs. Scripture also relates conflicts over *religious* issues, often including the *cultural* issues surrounding the tension. In describing the conflict that arose over how food was distributed to widows in Acts 6, Luke included the significant note that the two groups were culturally different, Greek and Hebrew.

Culture is not the same as "the world." In the New Testament, "world" is used in at least two ways. One is the physical world, the realm of human existence; an example is John 3:16, "For God so loved the world."* A second use is as the kingdom of this world, or the spirit of the

---

*All Scripture quotations in this chapter are from the NRSV.

world, that is in opposition to Christ and the kingdom of God (see John 8:23; James 4:4).

Every person in the world lives within a cultural group that uses the God-given capacity to develop how best to live, to deliver babies, to grow, to live acceptably within the world as part of that group. The mission of God sends the church out among the peoples of the world.

THE GOSPEL: CHALLENGING EVERY CULTURE

The biblical text carefully delineates Jesus' family heritage. He was very much a part of his culture. Following his reading of the scroll at the synagogue, his hearers were perplexed, asking, "Is not this the carpenter, the son of Mary and brother of James and Joses and Judas and Simon, and are not his sisters here with us?" (Mark 6:3). When someone goes outside the expectations of the culture (when someone hops over the cultural fences or fails to follow the cultural map), people take notice! From the beginning of his public ministry, Jesus not only challenged aspects of his own culture but also made way for the gospel to challenge every culture.

The Gospels record a number of occasions when Jesus forcefully rebuked the long-held traditions that hindered others from true worship and faithfully loving God. Jesus is an example to us that the most effective challenges to cultural maps come from the people who own, know, and use the map. Challenges to the wrongs of a society are seldom effective when made by someone outside the group.

God *can* use those who read from a different map, who have allowed God to challenge their own wrong ways, to help to bring attention to others' maps. However, this is seldom done well because we too often assume the others' maps should be like our own. "If you just follow the routes shown on our maps, you'll like where it brings you." Road maps for California are no good in Saskatchewan. They may look as though they should fit, but they don't. It is a foolish traveler who expects one map for all places.

Expecting to follow one's own cultural map, no matter one's location, is self-centered; it also is *ethnocentric*. Cultural self-centeredness hinders God's mission. Ethnocentrism's most ugly face is *racism*. It not only insists on one's own map but purposely excludes those of other groups and other societies, because racism judges them to be incapable or unworthy of hearing the gospel. Racism hinders others from using their own cultural maps to come to Christ; it does not allow them the same undeserved place of grace we have been given. We may try to hide racism in gracious terms: "We've got to be good stewards of our property." But racism is ugly and has no resemblance to the heart of God revealed in the *missio Dei.*

The missional church, participating in the *missio Dei,* always is careful to insist that the *gospel* challenges cultures. The ever-present danger is for the church to weaken the gospel challenge by judging others from its own cultural perspectives. Doing so violates the example of Jesus. The gospel, therefore, is always offensive, in every culture. The problem in cross-cultural ministry is that we often offend people culturally, so they never hear the offense of the gospel. We must be careful to offend people for the *right* (gospel) reasons, not the *wrong* (cultural) ones!

Don't offend unnecessarily for the wrong reasons!

THE GOSPEL: TRANSFORMING ALL CULTURES

Starting with the Holy Land of Jesus' day, when members of a society hear the good news and respond, Christ brings the light of the gospel to shine on cultural maps. The gospel brings sin into the light; it reveals prejudices and injustices. Powerful systems that oppose God and exploit people are challenged in profound ways.

Perhaps no story of the transformation of cultures by the gospel is more amazing than the story of St. Patrick of Ireland. At age sixteen, Patrick was kidnapped from his home in northeast England and sold as a slave to a landowner in Ireland. There Patrick served his new master as a shepherd. As Patrick drew on his Christian upbringing, God became real to him in the remote, lonely pastures, where he had ample time to pray. After six years God opened the way for Patrick to escape and return to his home. More than twenty years later God spoke to Patrick, who was now a parish priest. God called him to return to Ireland, this time as a missionary.

George Hunter III describes the results of Patrick's mission. In less than thirty years, the Irish were transformed from a people following a primal religion led by Druid priests, to a well-established indigenous form of Christianity. More than thirty of Ireland's one hundred fifty Celtic tribes had become substantially Christian.[3]

And the gospel continues to transform cultures. *eg. "Peace-Child"*

THE INCARNATION: FINDING THE *MISSIO DEI* AMONG THE WORLD'S PEOPLES

In the mission of God among the peoples of the world, Jesus becomes the example to show us how to participate. The triune God, Creator and Sustainer of the universe, became one of us in the person of the Son. The self-emptying of Jesus described in Philippians 2:7 gives us a powerful model of how God enables us to carry out God's mission in the world.

When Jesus wanted to communicate God's desire that all come to know, love, and worship God, he did so by first setting aside his cultural map; he "did not regard equality with God as something to be exploited, but emptied himself, taking the form [map, culture] of a slave [servant]" (Phil. 2:6-7). The customs of the society into which Jesus was born became his customs. Jesus learned to speak Aramaic with what some today might call a "hillbilly accent," instead of the more prestigious accent spoken in Jerusalem. He did not require humans to learn God's language to understand God's message. *XForce unnec. cultural elements for own Culture*

The Incarnation shows us the value God places on people, that God would value humanity to the point of such self-sacrifice. It shows us this value by the limitations Jesus assumed when he took on the culture of this very specific group of people. Yet, because Jesus did so in *that* society, we are assured the gospel can transform people of *every* society.

Wouldn't it have been better to expand the mission, to proclaim the day of salvation to the whole region around the Mediterranean, or even the then known world? Wouldn't this have been more effective, and more efficient, than focusing on one small, seemingly insignificant group of people? Apparently God didn't think so.

It is easy to speak of the Incarnation in ways we have come to value highly: self-giving, emptying, serving. Actually following the example is much more difficult. We admire self-sacrifice when others do it but may find that even the small sacrifices are difficult when we are called to

Meaning of sacrifice.

make them. Yet throughout the world, brothers and sisters in Christ are daily called to make the ultimate sacrifice. In doing so, they follow Jesus' incarnation.

In participating in the mission of God, the missional church is called to make the cultural sacrifice. We are not asked to forsake our own cultural maps but, just as Jesus did, to lay them aside in honor of entering into the life of others so they may experience the kingdom of God in *their* day in, day out living. The missional church embraces the mission of God by living incarnationally among the cultures of the world.

THE MISSIONAL CHURCH: SEEKING THE UNCOMMON RELATIONSHIP

Rather than going to those most like us, the missional church intentionally embraces cultural differences. Andrew Walls notes that the advances of Christianity generally occur at the peripheries of societies. Thus, Christianity continually interacts creatively with new cultures.[4] Local churches are not to be afraid of encountering the society around them or beyond them. Rather than seeing the differences that may exist between the local church and its surrounding context, the church sees that by following the pattern of Christian history and engaging cultures for Christ, it embraces the *missio Dei*.

Keith Schwanz describes interfacing at the peripheries with those who have different cultural maps as "the church seeking uncommon relationships." He illustrates this from his own experience:

> I met Paco on a Sunday evening. From the first moment, I knew Paco faced many challenges in his life. His gestures were exaggerated and could be alarming to the timid. He didn't sit still for long, but throughout the worship service was up and down, in and out. Paco found acceptance, however, and a family, with the people of El Buen Samaritano in Guadalajara, Mexico.
>
> Dr. Jorge Cordova was the founding pastor of El Buen Samaritano. He also was a medical doctor who often ministered to the street people of Guadalajara. He was known in the neighborhood as a man who would help anyone in need. I knew immediately Paco

was one with whom Jorge had shared the love of Jesus; Jorge was Paco's friend.

On the following Wednesday evening, several of us were headed to a telephone booth on a street corner in downtown Guadalajara. As we stepped out of the hotel lobby, we saw Paco pacing the sidewalk. Paco saw us, too, and remembered us. Arms waving and body jerking, Paco hurried over to our group. He gave me a big hug. Any friend of Jorge was a friend of Paco!

As we embraced, I noticed a taxi driver leaning on the front fender of his taxi, totally baffled by what he had just seen. His eyes were opened wide as could be. Why was an American tourist hugging a Mexican street person in downtown Guadalajara?

Christians are called to embody the love of Jesus, and this love will transcend economic, cultural, and racial identities, not orbit around one of them. God is glorified in uncommon relationships.[5]

THE CULMINATION:
GOD INVITES THE CHURCH TO MISSION

As the missional church lives the incarnational life of Christ among the peoples of the world, it becomes aware of its own cultural bias, its own ethnocentrism. If the gospel is to transform a people, it must be allowed to take up its home in that new culture. The message is enculturated as its messengers give up the rights to insist on their own cultural maps and delight to see the gospel go deep into the most fundamental ways that others see the world. The Spirit revealed to John what God intends as the culmination of the *missio Dei,* "After this I looked, and there was a great multitude that no one could count, from every nation, from all tribes and peoples and languages, standing before the throne and before the Lamb, robed in white, with palm branches in their hands. They cried out in a loud voice, saying, 'Salvation belongs to our God who is seated on the throne, and to the Lamb!'" (Rev. 7:9-10).

The gospel not only affirms the rich variety of the cultures of the world but also challenges all cultures. But it does so not on the basis of any one culture. The kingdom of God in its fullness will be multinational, multiclan, and multilingual, kaleidoscopic beyond imagination.

Until then, finding a place to be missional isn't difficult. As related in the Preface to this volume, Pastor Mark found a missional context for himself and his congregation right across the street. Among the people of our own society is the place to begin to find the *missio Dei* and the place to begin being missional. Then the Spirit of God continues to send the missional church out to peoples of further and further peripheries—from Jerusalem, to Judea and all Samaria, to the ends of the earth. Are you ready?

PART III

PARTICIPATING IN THE
MISSIO DEI

14

WORSHIP
THE HEARTBEAT OF MISSIONAL LIVING
Keith Schwanz

━━━━━━━━━━━━━━━◆━━━━━━━━━━━━━━━

Systole . . . diastole. Contraction . . . expansion. Out . . . in. The rhythmic beat of the heart pushes blood out of the chambers . . . then draws more in. Beyond conscious awareness, unless the rhythm is off-kilter or the blood pressure cuff is strapped on an arm, the heart does its work of circulating nutrients and oxygen throughout the body and carrying waste and carbon dioxide to be disposed.

Similarly, God designed a rhythm of worship. Out . . . in. Impelled by love, the "peculiar people" (1 Pet. 2:9, KJV) respond to God's call to embody God's mission of reconciliation to the world. On the Sabbath, the day of rest and renewal, God's people assemble in praise and confession. Sending . . . gathering. Both exhibit God's mission; both express worship.

The writer of Hebrews noted this rhythm of worship: the sacrifices of sharing, and the sacrifice of praise. "Through him, then, let us continually offer a sacrifice of praise to God, that is, the fruit of lips that confess his name. Do not neglect to do good and to share what you have, for such sacrifices are pleasing to God" (13:15-16).*

The outward actions, the sacrifices of good deeds, require a discernment of God's mission and a decision to participate in what God is doing in the world. This involves cooperation with God. It would be absurd to praise God for God's mighty acts but refuse to participate in God's mission, either because of neglect or opposition to God's way. Worship as a response to God involves doing good.

---

*All Scripture quotations in this chapter are from the NRSV, except as noted.

The upward action, the sacrifice of praise, includes describing God's actions and character. Through this fellowship with God, the gathered people express their gratitude for God's actions and align themselves, both corporately and individually, with God's character. This requires a commitment to God. Worship as a response to God involves praise and petition, proclamation and transformation.

GOD'S STORY

The rhythm of worship in a missional congregation provides God's people an orientation to God's story. Just as a sunflower in bud stage on the Kansas plains orients itself to the sun, so the body of Christ finds its reference point in the story of God's redemptive acts.

N. T. Wright, a leading New Testament scholar, stated, "The biblical story from Genesis to Revelation is a great drama, a great saga, a play written by the living God and staged in his wonderful creation; and in liturgy, whether or not sacramental, we become for a moment not only spectators of this play but also willing participants in it. It is not our play; it is God's play, and we are not free to rewrite the script."[1] In worship, then, God's story must be told as fully as possible.

Some people promote a song-driven worship, but in the process unwittingly minimize how much of God's story can be considered. Since a hymn exists in a compact art form, constrained by meter and rhythm and rhyme, a minuscule part of God's story can be told in one hymn, even if the hymn takes the congregation toward a textual climax. Many praise songs used today state only one thing, so even less of God's story is recounted than with a hymn. Instead of song-driven worship, if we are to tell God's story faithfully we need Scripture-infused worship. "We cannot read the whole Bible in each worship service, but the selections we choose, whether through a lectionary or not, should reflect the larger story and remind us of its full sweep and flow."[2]

In telling God's story, sometimes we speak about God to ourselves, proclaiming the majesty and mercy of God. Other times we speak about God to God, praising God for God's holiness and love. When we locate our stories within God's story, sometimes we speak about ourselves to ourselves, affirming that we are God's people. Other times we speak about ourselves to God, *petitioning* God to be gracious. In these various modes of communication we tell the story of God's mission to bring us and the world under God's reign.   *Worship : Response to God*

Worship located in God's mission is a response to God's gracious action, not the result of human initiative. Nothing we do can get out in front of God, but some worship planners try. Some have viewed worship as merely preparation for mission. In this case the preacher or song leader seeks to inspire people to share the good news with those outside the church. Worship and mission do not interact in this case; the hope is that the worshippers will get excited enough to share the gospel with their friends. Others see worship primarily as a means for mission. The preacher encourages the people to bring seekers to the gatherings in hopes that the seekers will choose to follow Christ. In both of these scenarios, worship is used as a way by which something else is accomplished. The worship leaders, in these instances, seek to motivate (and manipulate?) so as to produce the desired emotional or behavioral response. For these worship leaders it is a travesty if a worship event is boring or mediocre because that will be unlikely to achieve the desired, but distorted, result.

The misguided preacher or worship leader who relies on dynamism and charisma seeks to "act upon" the worshippers. Stanley Hauerwas, a theologian and ethicist, warned that "the difficulty with worship intentionally shaped to entertain those who are 'new' is not that it is entertaining but that the god that is entertained in such worship cannot be the Trinity."[3] If the spotlight rests on people, then the beam is directed wrongly, even if the motivation is honorable. For the missional church, in contrast, the worship leader is not concerned about what he does *to* the ← congregation in hopes that they *might* encounter God, but what he helps the congregation to do because they *have encountered God*. From first to last, worship should tell the story of the Alpha and Omega and not stoop to anything less lofty. The mission of God precedes all human initiative, including worship practices.

In a missional congregation, the task of a worship leader begins by discerning the *missio Dei* as expressed in the congregation's context. Sensitivity to and reflection on God's activity goes before all other actions of a worship planner. Further, the worship planner must be pastoral, observing how the encounters with God transform the people who look to her for spiritual guidance. Once she begins to discern how God is at work among the congregation, then she helps the congregation give voice to the glory of what God is doing in their midst. In this way the congregation joins what God initiated.

GOD'S FORMING OF A PEOPLE

Part of the mission of God involves forming a redeemed people who seek the reconciliation of the world through Christ. Peter, in writing to scattered believers, reminded them that they were "a chosen race, a royal priesthood, a holy nation, God's own people, in order that you may proclaim the mighty acts of him who called you out of darkness into his marvelous light" (1 Pet. 2:9). Their very existence as the people of God proclaimed God's light. "The church . . . not only has a story to tell but is itself the reality and embodiment of the story. It is the very presence of the Missio Dei."[4] The church exists to be and live as God intends, a microcosm of God's plan for the whole world.

When people assemble for corporate worship, they give evidence of the mission of God in forming a people. "The gathering of a people to witness to and participate in this reconciling movement of God toward the world is an integral part of God's mission. The visible act of assembly (in Christ by the power of the Spirit) and the forms of this assembly—what we call liturgy—enact and signify this mission."[5] As the congregation draws together through the enactment of God's story, the worship centers them on "the grace of the Lord Jesus Christ, and the love of God, and the fellowship of the Holy Spirit" (2 Cor. 13:14, NIV). Worship deepens and extends their understanding of and commitment to living in the way of Jesus.

The Greek root for the word "synagogue" means "to gather," signifying a public meeting. Likewise, the Greek word often used for the church, *ekklesia,* means a public gathering. The church is always the gathered people and worship is a public act. By contrast, Darrell Guder has reminded us, "Our postmodern society has come to regard worship as the private, internal, and often arcane activity of religionists who retreat from the world to practice their mystical rites." Guder emphasized the public character of worship and reiterated that for the *ekklesia* "its worship is its first form of mission."[6] Even in the simple gathering of God's people, before anyone speaks a word, the story of God's mission to reconcile the world becomes evident. The first public witness of God is the character and nature of the body gathered in Jesus' name. The witness of the congregation advances even further as the people serve one another, honor one another, encourage one another, and bear one another's burdens.

The practice of some people to remain anonymous in worship, to slip in at the last minute and leave before the congregation receives the benediction, thwarts God's desire to form a people and makes worship as mission less effective. A growing number of traveling musicians characterize their concerts as times of worship. To gather with thousands of people unknown to each other causes worship to be disembodied from the ongoing shared life of the community. The worshipper stands in isolation all the while God intends the community to form the witness. In contrast to this, Lesslie Newbigin observes, "As we share in the life and worship of the Church, through fellowship, word, and sacrament, we indwell the story and from within that story we seek to be the voice and the hands of Jesus for our time and place."[7] Anything less than a vibrant community of believers who share life together dwarfs God's intention for worship in the missional church.

Just as early drafts of a novel may have "plot holes," so a congregation's telling of God's story may have practices inconsistent with that narrative. Some leaders corrupt worship through an emphasis on self-interests, such as need-meeting ministries or seeking after emotional experiences. Others promote institutional interests such as a building program, a financial campaign, or an attendance drive, and call it worship. If worship is about God's story, but an action causes a congregation to focus elsewhere, then it is not true worship. Authentic worship occurs when God's people proclaim and participate in God's story.

The cultural context of a group of Jesus' followers must be considered in the discussion of worship and mission. "God did not create facsimiles. He did not establish His kingdom on earth by using industrial molds. God always creates and uses originals: matchless human beings and matchless communities, gathered to honor Him at a certain point on the time line and a certain point on the globe."[8] The particularity of a congregation will influence decisions made about how to assist the congregation most effectively in giving voice to its praise of God and in prompting its actions as participants in God's mission.

The context, for example, will inform decisions made about the style of worship, especially the idiom of music used in corporate worship. But the context is a poor place to begin the worship planning. Robert Webber, a prolific author on worship, often wrote about content, structure, and style.[9] As discussed in this chapter, the content of worship must be thoroughly saturated in the biblical story of God's redemptive actions. Content takes precedence; structure and style serve content in worship. The structure must enhance the telling of God's story, allowing the congregation to engage and enact the story. Thinking theologically about the structure of worship,[10] the congregation gathers as a visible witness of God's redemptive mission, they are formed, reformed, and transformed as they engage God's story, and, finally, the centrifugal movement of the triune God compels them to embody and proclaim the gospel as scattered seed in God's garden. This theological construct is parallel to the classic structure of worship: gathering, Word and sacrament, and sending. This structure serves the content (God's story) and works in any style. Style is determined by the cultural context in which the worship gathering exists. Webber wrote that style "is a matter of making the content and structure of worship *indigenous* to the local setting."[11] Style most often is primarily about the type of music used in the service. The words of a song must be selected because of how they contribute to the telling of God's story; the music of a song should be in an idiom familiar to the worshippers.

Many worship leaders begin with style, seeking first to determine what the people like, thus treating the worshippers as consumers of religious services. Newbigin, a leading voice in the missional church conversation, contended that "authentic Christian thought and action begin not by attending to the aspirations of the people, not by answering the questions they are asking in their terms, not by offering solutions to the problems as the world sees them. It must begin and continue by attending to what God has done in the story of Israel and supremely in the story of Jesus Christ. It must continue by indwelling that story so that it is our story,

Priorities: Content → Structure → Style

the way we understand the real story."[12] In authentic worship the leader gives priority to consideration of God's mission, which informs content (God's story, as in the Newbigin quote above) and structure ("indwelling that story"), then reflects on how the context informs the style.

Worship determined primarily by the context does not generate missional people. Starting with the context would be like looking in a rearview mirror, staring at yourself, the toddler in the car seat, and the road you've already traveled. Instead of staring backward at the context, the wise worship leader seeks to discern God's mission, to look through the windshield in search of evidence of God's eternal reign.

WORSHIP'S CONTINUOUS CYCLE: OUTWARD . . . UPWARD

The Greek word from which we get our English word "liturgy," *leitourgia*, literally means the "work of the people." The action of the assembly is its liturgy, whether in formal or informal expressions. In its original usage, however, *leitourgia* also signified "work *for* the people." In the ancient Greek and Roman world, for example, wealthy citizens provided, at their own expense, services for the public good—work for the people. Rodney Clapp notes, "The Eastern Orthodox helpfully speak of mission as 'liturgy after the liturgy' . . . Mission is the 'work of the people' Monday through Saturday, done after and formed by the 'work of the people' on the first day, Sunday."[13] Worship always looks out after it looks up.

Sally Morgenthaler flipped the order—outward . . . upward—when she suggested, "The creation of sacred space starts 'out there'—beyond our four walls—not 'in here.' If we can't create sacred space out there (that is, connecting with our neighbors, coworkers, and imperfect strangers in our everyday routines), then whatever we do on Sunday or on Wednesday night will ring hollow, even if we have all the bells and whistles."[14] This indicated a dramatic shift in Morgenthaler's understanding of worship and mission. In her book *Worship Evangelism* (1995), Morgenthaler argued that congregations should update worship styles to be more enticing to the person unfamiliar with Christianity. Twelve years later, no longer seeing worship as an attraction to the nonchurch person, she became "convinced that the primary meeting place with our unchurched friends is now outside the church building. Worship must finally become, as Paul reminds us, more life than event (Romans 12:1-2)."[15]

JOHN WESLEY AND THE MEANS OF GRACE

John Wesley preached a sermon on the means of grace, that is, the outward signs, words, or actions by which a person experiences God's transforming grace. Wesley began his argument by declaring that God is the author of grace. A "stupid, senseless wretch" with no interest in God suddenly becomes aware of God's initiative and invitation. As the person responds to God, the means of grace become the ongoing expression of the spiritual encounter God initiated.

Toward the end of the sermon, Wesley provided specific directions and warnings.

- *God is above all means.* God is the initiator in the spiritual encounter. God is the first witness; human effort is always a subsequent witness.
- *There is no power in the means.* As exciting as the music may feel or as inspiring as a preacher may be, there is no power apart from the Spirit of God already at work. The pastor who guarantees a church board that congregational renewal and growth will come if they change worship style has promised too much.
- *In using all means, seek God alone.* Music, drama, and preaching are performing arts and often draw attention to the performer. Some worship leaders relish the spotlight. The worship team member, however, who equates spiritual vitality with musical excellence and emotional thrill expects too little. Seek God who is above all means, Wesley urged.[16]

"The goal of liturgy is to immerse God's people in God's gospel story in such a way that this people will be able to live out the mission of Jesus in their everyday lives."[17] Only as worshippers embody and enact the gospel—both in everyday life and as a gathering community—will the worship be missional.

Sending . . . gathering. Out . . . in. The heartbeat of worship gives life to and invigorates the missional people of God.

15
A MISSIONAL CATECHESIS FOR FAITHFUL DISCIPLESHIP
Dean G. Blevins

What is the purpose of Sunday school or small groups? To evangelize unbelievers, or to shape and "nurture" members of the church? Often the wedge between evangelism and education forces ministers to accept one approach, leaving churches lacking either in witness or nurture. True, Christian educators embrace evangelism of the ages, preparing people to reach out to future generations. Christian education also serves evangelism by "conserving" and by creating new converts via small groups. Wesley himself employed this strategy in early Methodism. Unfortunately, some people today consider the mutual desire to evangelize and nurture congregants as competing interests.

INTRODUCTION

Regrettably, many people think evangelism works like a business deal where the evangelist offers the gospel in exchange for repentance and faith. People weigh the benefits or consequences of conversion against their old life. The "swap" is a one-time event and people often think they have completed their discipleship in a moment's decision. Christian educators often begin at the other extreme. They focus on long-term growth around age level issues. Unfortunately they also draw from a public school approach developed in the industrial era where students advance like a production line on the conveyor belt of education. Grade by grade they put together knowledge like parts on a car. Students often graduate "from" high school and graduate "out" of the church. Single decision evangelism or production line education leaves church members with a limited discipleship.

We need a different understanding of discipleship, one that calls for an ongoing commitment based less on our "arrival" as Christians and more on God's mission in the world. Adopting a missional approach that

from the early church's understanding of _catechesis_ (religious
n) is a strategy designed to follow God's gospel.

TURNING TOWARD MISSIONAL DISCIPLESHIP

Discipleship calls for a lifelong journey after Jesus. Wesleyan discipleship seeks to transform people and churches toward holiness of heart
and life.[1] Anchored in Jesus' ministry with his disciples, the process includes an apprenticeship to the Holy Spirit. We learn to live out God's
kingdom "on earth as it is in heaven" (Matt. 6:10, NRSV).

The missional church believes God sends the church into the world
and quickly discovers a God already at work! Missional engagement is
more than evangelistic outreach and can include compassionate activity,
community development, and social justice. John Wesley called these
practices "works of mercy." Collectively these acts "witness" the grace of
God through Jesus Christ by the power of the Holy Spirit.

Researchers have recently identified the main characteristics of missionally minded congregations. A missional church:

1. Proclaims the gospel.
2. Is a community where all members are involved in learning to
   become disciples of Jesus.
3. [Accepts the Bible as] normative in this church's life.
4. Understands itself as different from the world because of its participation in the life, death, and resurrection of its Lord.
5. Seeks to discern God's specific missional vocation for the entire
   community and for all its members.
6. Is known by how its members behave toward one another.
7. Practices reconciliation.
8. Teaches and encourages its members to hold themselves ac-
   countable to one another in love.
9. Practices hospitality.
10. Accepts worship as the central act by which the community
    celebrates with joy and thanksgiving God's presence and God's
    promised future.
11. Possesses a vital public witness.

12. Recognizes the church itself is an incomplete expression of the reign of God.[2]

These core characteristics show that missional churches emphasize engagement but also include basic formation. Churches combine proclamation, reconciliation, hospitality, and witness with worship, accountability, Scripture study, and discernment. Without returning to the evangelism/education divide, can we be missional and shape Christians? Perhaps "catechesis" shows the way.

EARLY CHURCH CATECHESIS

The idea of catechesis may conjure up small catechism booklets or membership materials. These texts contained routine Q&A sessions over the Bible and basic doctrine. Originally rote learning, catechesis is more than indoctrination. John Westerhoff notes the word has a rich church heritage. Though a membership process, catechesis includes any intentional, pastoral process that shapes "belief, becoming, and behavior" in community.[3] Obviously, the early church did not have a uniform approach. What we do know from early church writers, however, provides insight through some common similarities. The early church pastor Hippolytus focused not only on knowledge but also on lifestyle.[4] Hippolytus asked sponsors to give an account for candidates' lives when new members came up for church membership.[5] Prospective church members needed to model Christian living before they were considered to fully know doctrine. Christians had to live closely *with* unbelievers until the unbelievers could testify to their character and behavior. Undoubtedly, candidates learned about faithful living through the explanation and example of Christians who met them in their homes, their work spaces, and their lives. As the early church grew, many people (called catechumens) attended congregations for several years without becoming full members. Those who joined went through a deliberate (catechetical) process. This process involved intense instruction, public baptism, and post-baptism education.

No church leader was better at catechesis than Augustine of Hippo. First, Augustine drew from the culture of his day. Influenced by Greco-Roman public speaking (oratory) Augustine's preaching appealed to people who appreciated the spoken word in law, politics, and entertainment. Preaching was a "public" act much like people today going to a movie or play. Orators provided the same information and entertainment as radio, television, and computers today. Preaching drew people for many reasons. Nevertheless, Augustine based his oratory on God's Word. He considered speech-making frivolous without the gospel. Augustine preached passages in depth. He always included the broader, biblical story of God. The Bible revealed both the love of God and our need to love others. Preaching was a cultural adaptation of oratory where the message transformed ordinary entertainment into God's mission.[6]

Second, Augustine understood the learner during initial evangelism and later discipleship. He recognized that people came with different expectations. The bishop adapted his approach based on people's education, their opposition or acceptance of Scripture, and their familiarity with the local church. Augustine connected Scripture to the life of the listener. As people became catechumens, Augustine stressed God's majesty through the book of John. He taught believers that the Psalms were the very heart of God. Augustine offered a deliberate process that transformed believers into love of God and love of neighbor.[7]

There were three catechetical stages or groups in the early church and in Augustine's ministry.[8] The first group of people was known as "hearers." They stayed in the worship service through the sermon but left before community prayers or the Lord's Supper. Augustine emphasized the gospel through the "public" act of preaching.

The second group, called petitioners or kneelers, went through an intense discipleship during Lent. The process was both personal and deeply communal. Augustine focused on faith and works. These works were an extension of God's love, including personal conduct, a simple lifestyle, and care of the poor.

Petitioners "renounced the devil and recited the Creed" prior to baptism. Renunciation, a public act, reflected a total turn from evil and toward God. This commitment did not end the power of sin. Petitioners continued to learn how to discipline their desires. Renunciation was a radical movement to follow Christ. Petitioners also recited the Apostles' Creed. More than a summary of faith, Augustine hoped the creed served as a doorway into Scripture. Petitioners also learned the Lord's Prayer as a description of life in the kingdom of God.

Finally, the third group, the baptized, were known as "risen" or "faithful" members. Augustine was careful not to allow new members to think their journey was over. Catechesis included learning the meaning of baptism and the Lord's Supper. He remarked how the Communion bread symbolizes the bread of life we need for the ongoing journey. Augustine taught baptism as an initiation, not an ending. Baptism symbolized passing through the Red Sea, with the Promised Land yet to come. Marked by baptism, these "risen" members possess the spiritual food of communion for the journey.[9]

MISSIONAL CATECHESIS

John Westerhoff says, "By catechesis we assert every activity used by the church to celebrate and imitate the word or actions of God."[10] So what does it mean to celebrate and imitate a *missional* God today? Missionally reframing the three catechetical movements of hearing, kneeling, and rising provides a better understanding.

Hearing Gospel and Culture

Augustine understood that catechesis began by presenting the gospel clearly. Different people could engage the story of God through conversation and proclamation. No doubt "hearing" and finding ourselves within the story of God forms personal and community identities. Augustine understood the power of Scripture. He dedicated his ministry to clearly proclaiming this story, inviting congregants and catechumens alike to "lean into" the story. Yet Augustine assumed that the Bible would be read "in light of the commandment of love of God and neighbor."[11] As Wesley might state it, Scripture invites faith, but it also perfects faith into love.

Yet Augustine also teaches us to "hear" local culture. Augustine remained deeply aware of his culture, including current events.[12] True, Augustine did contrast local culture with the "City of God," however, he encouraged church members to live faithfully in this world while awaiting

Jesus' return.[13] Augustine used the rhetorical culture of his day to define God's work and to call the church to live the gospel.

We must learn to listen carefully to culture, to "hear" the rhythms of individual lives and neighborhood life. At times our listening will critique practices that privilege the rich or impede the poor, a criticism shared by Wesley.[14] We also need to listen carefully to where God also may be at work *through culture.* This allows us to discover community activities that work for the sake of the gospel. Learning to listen both to the gospel and to culture remains a lifelong challenge for discipleship. No wonder this task provides the first step into a missional catechesis.

Kneeling in Prayer and Service

Second, missional catechesis focuses on the conversion of people and of communities. Augustine emphasized the need for radical conversion, a public commitment to a new way of life. Candidates at this phase knelt in prayer in church and in obedience during the training period of Lent. Discipleship included obedience and a change in character. It also included embracing the faith (the Apostles' Creed) and praying the prayer that shapes the kingdom of God.

Yet praying the Lord's Prayer's petition "Thy kingdom come, Thy will be done" invites the kneeler to embrace God's missional desire to see the kingdom break into everyday life. Augustine understood this principle through his emphasis on faith and works. We kneel before Christ in prayer but also remember Christ's kneeling with towel and basin (John 13:1-17). We respond to obedience through service. Engaging the local community in prayerful service also calls us to "convert" community structures and needs. Our efforts in neighborhoods force us to examine our faith. We turn to the Apostles' Creed as a living document that gives meaning and purpose to our efforts. We live out the Lord's Prayer in our service to others.

A missional catechesis understands that the call to follow God is a call to serve God as a particular, loving people. We serve out of a distinctive Christian perspective. Our engagement with society becomes a continual journey of action and reflection.[15] Discipleship continues as service calls us to faith and prayer, even while faith and prayer lead us back to service.

Rising: Baptism and the Commissioned Life

Undoubtedly, in baptism one identifies fully with the lordship of Christ and with the church, the body of Christ. Kneelers now rise to new life (Rom. 6:4). Augustine called them "new children" in Christ.[16] Newly baptized members joined the final phase of worship, the celebration of the Lord's Supper. Communion services were more than bread and cup. New members learned practices that said they belonged: new greetings, the kiss of peace, and new prayers. The Lord's Supper meant reliving the most powerful moments of the life, death, and resurrection of Jesus. John Wesley encouraged Methodists to participate frequently in the Lord's Supper. He also encouraged them to remember their baptism through a New Year's covenant service.

Augustine (and Wesley) understood that even this phase of discipleship includes ministry beyond the practice of the church. Augustine reminded these "young" believers not to neglect the poor, but to live the faith through acts of mercy.[17] Augustine understood that the church lives "in-between" Christ's first appearance and his ultimate return. It is not enough just to join the church since the work of the church is not yet complete. As noted, the Lord's Supper provides food for the journey after God's missional heart.

A missional catechesis also takes seriously that joining the church becomes our commission to follow God beyond the walls of the church. Missiologist Lesslie Newbigin noted new believers—indeed, all church members—are commissioned as priests to the world.[18] John Wesley also understood that Methodists (and all Christians) should live out the kingdom of God as a community of people.[19] Sent by God, the church serves as a means of grace, both in the shaping of new believers and following God's mission into the world.

CONCLUSION

Missional catechesis provides a discipleship that overcomes the evangelism/education divide. Formation and engagement work together at every phase of discipleship. We listen for God at work in Scripture and in the world. We kneel to allow ourselves to be transformed. We also kneel to serve as transformational agents in the world, following Christ's sacrificial service. We rise to enter the community of faith only to find ourselves "commissioned," sent out into the world where God is at work. Through this process we realize our discipleship never ends primarily because the missional God who calls us also commends us to God's missional heart. A missional catechesis resonates with our Wesleyan tradition, pointing us toward God's future, both in the life of the church and in the world beyond.

16
KOINŌNIA
THE SHARING-OUT COMMUNITY
Judith A. Schwanz

◆

Social isolation and individualism. These twin realities pervade contemporary North American society. Over forty years ago Paul Simon and Art Garfunkel used the image of an island that never cries to symbolize social isolation. More recently, Harvard University professor Robert Putnam explored the impact of increasing isolation and individualism on society as a whole. In his book *Bowling Alone,* Putnam defined "social capital" as the "connections among individuals—social networks and the norms of reciprocity and trustworthiness that arise from them."[1] He studied a broad range of social networks: garden clubs, civic clubs, bowling leagues, Parent/Teacher Associations (PTAs), veterans organizations, and so on, and noted the decline (and even demise) of these social networks. Writing as a sociologist, Putnam called for renewed and creative approaches to building community and social capital. As people who seek to fulfill God's mission, we must take up that call and learn to create Christian communities where no one need feel he or she stands alone.

DESIGNED FOR RELATIONSHIP—SHARED LIFE

Loneliness brings pain both individually and socially because it violates our very nature. God created us for relationship. God said, "It is not good that the man should be alone; I will make him a helper as his partner" (Gen 2:18).*

---

*All Scripture quotations in this chapter are from the NRSV, except as noted.

Reuben Welch wrote a book based on 1 John, viewed through his experience as a chaplain at Pasadena Nazarene College. He titled the book *We Really Do Need Each Other.*[2] This message holds true for all people, not just college students: we cannot survive the journey through life in isolation.

Our hunger for relationship makes sense when we consider our Creator. The God who designed humankind for relationship also exists *in* relationship—God the Father/Creator, Son/Redeemer, and Holy Spirit/ Comforter. We hear signs of the Trinity in God's words at creation, "Let *us* make humankind in *our* image, according to *our* likeness" (Gen. 1:26, emphasis added). Stephen Seamands maintains that the Trinity "reveals that persons are essentially relational."[3] So as we seek to become more like Christ, to grow spiritually implies growing in community with other Christ followers.

The Christian community, the ekklesia, is "called out" to share life, to live in fellowship. An important Greek word used in the New Testament to describe the church is *koinōnia,* literally, "fellowship" or "community." Several years ago my husband and I became acquainted with about twenty young adults, both married and single, who all attended the same church. They met together weekly in someone's home as a "Life Group." Having heard the frightening statistics about the shrinking numbers of young adults who stay in the church following college, we asked if we could meet with the group. We posed the question, "Why are you in church when so many of your peers have left?" Their answers resounded with one common theme: relationships. These young men and women had found *koinōnia* with each other as they sought together to become more like Christ.

The missional church lives out *koinōnia* in response to Peter's assertion that we are God's chosen people (1 Pet. 2:9). We recognize that God designed human persons *for* community. God has called us to work together as partners in the gospel (Phil. 1). We bear the image of God (Gen. 1:26); the purpose of an image is to represent the original. God's mission for us is to represent God-in-relationship on the earth, to live *koinōnia* in God's image. Jesus commanded his disciples, "Just as I have loved you, you also should love one another. By this everyone will know that you

Known by LOVE

are my disciples, if you have love for one another" (John 13:34*b*-35). Our love for each other reflects God's love for us.

KOINŌNIA AS INTENTIONAL SHARED LIFE

True *koinōnia* doesn't just happen; we build community *intentionally.* Without intentional effort, we will drift back into our culturally conditioned default of isolation and individualism. For many of us, that is all we've known even while we have hungered for connection. We need to learn and deliberately choose to seek out deeper relationships with others.

The missional church seeks to build *koinōnia* through the practice of hospitality—of making room for others. In our individualistic society we tend to think of hospitality as inviting others into our private homes for a special meal or as pampered overnight guests. This type of hospitality often becomes formal, expensive, and burdensome, thus limited in scope. True hospitality includes making room in our homes, but it focuses on *relationships* with guests, not on abundance of fine food or quality of accommodations.

True hospitality also includes creating space for others in our hearts, in our minds, and in our schedules as *companions*. The first part of this word, *com,* means "together"; the second part, *panion,* is from the Latin word for "bread." Literally, to "companion" with someone signifies to share bread, to eat together. When we sit down with another person at a table for a meal, or even a cup of coffee, something special happens. The quality of our sharing deepens as we take time with each other. When we companion together over a meal, the table service and food are not the primary focus; they merely serve the purpose of making space to connect with the people with whom we share. We make space in our hearts for others, caring about their concerns, rejoicing in their victories, learning their thoughts and dreams.

In Scripture, breaking bread together signified reconciliation or restoration of relationship. After Laban chased down the departing Jacob and his family, the relatives all sat down to a meal together as a gesture of goodwill (Gen. 31:54). Conversely, in the story of the prodigal son, the older brother refused to extend hospitality, to come into the house and eat with his returned sibling (Luke 15:28).

When we experience *koinōnia,* fellowship that images or represents God, members of the community share life together. We create a safe, grace-filled place where we can take off our masks and share our true selves with each other. This may not always look pretty and polished; *koinōnia* centers on relationships, not appearances. Darrell Guder has stated that missional communities "representing the reign of God will be intentional about providing the space, the time, and the resources for people to unlearn old patterns and learn new ways of living that reveal God's transforming and healing power."[4] We learn how to live under the reign of God *together,* which requires time and space as we open our hearts to make room for each other.

KOINŌNIA AS REFLECTIVE SHARED LIFE

The fellowship to which God calls us also entails a life of reflection. As we consider our life shared together in community, we find "spiritual meaning in ordinary practices, such as hospitality or friendship, and in normal life-cycle occurrences, like birth, sexual love, sickness, and death. The quality of any relationship is all important, and each is capable of transcendent meaning."[5] Elizabeth O'Connor has written about the Church of the Saviour, a missional community in Washington, D.C. Members of this fellowship identified five "marks" of a liberating community. Two of the marks highlight the importance of reflection: "a radical commitment to a critical contemplation of one's own life and the life of one's faith community" and "commitment to a life of reflection . . . In reflection the emotional and the intellectual become partners."[6]

The missional church reflects, seeking to discern where God already is working and joining in God's mission. That requires "pondering in our hearts" as Mary, the mother of Jesus, did following the shepherds' visit (Luke 2:19). We reflect individually on our own lives and corporately on our life together. Reflection takes us beyond "what we do" to asking "why we do what we do." Reflection also takes us deeper from questions about what we should *do* to questions about who we should *be.*

KOINŌNIA AS DIVERSE SHARED LIFE

The fellowship that reflects God's image to the world allows for and thrives on diversity. In Paul's words to the Galatians, "As many of you as were baptized into Christ have clothed yourselves with Christ. There is no longer Jew or Greek, there is no longer slave or free, there is no longer male and female; for all of you are one in Christ Jesus" (3:27-28). God's mission calls men and women of all races and from all walks of life. The missional community seeks to reflect this diversity among its members. The community actually becomes stronger as we learn to deal with the internal and external resistance that naturally results between members of the fellowship who differ from one another.

Over a half century ago W. Ross Ashby wrote *An Introduction to Cybernetics,*[7] the study of the structure of regulatory systems. Ashby's work focused primarily on technical and mechanical systems. However, since his writing, scientists who study living systems have demonstrated the applicability of general systems principles to human systems and organizations such as the church.

Ashby introduced the law of requisite variety. In essence, Ashby's law states that to be adaptable to a variable environment a system must have a variety of responses available to it. Thus, the greater the variety (diversity) within a system, the more variety (change) the system can handle in its environment. Alan Hirsch stated that when a system "has generally not cultivated adaptability and internal variety, it will ultimately deteriorate toward equilibrium. And in living systems total equilibrium means death."[8] As members of the missional church, we must embrace those who look, think, and act different from us rather than seeking a homogenous unit. The only necessary common factor in our fellowship would be our desire to follow Jesus and pursue God's mission in the world.

We live in a world of increasing diversity and options. If the church chooses to huddle inside our buildings and interact only with others who look and talk just like us, we will lose any ability to minister to the society around us. We must reach out—get out of our buildings and live life with people whose differences from us will stretch us.

SHARED-OUT LIFE

In 2 Corinthians 9:13 Paul spoke of *koinōnia* to describe the contribution or offering that the Corinthians had taken for relief for the poor. The word *koinōnia* used by itself never meant "contribution,"[9] but in this particular biblical context it indicates a "sharing-out attitude." The believers' participation in this demonstration of care for the poor demonstrated the reality of their faith confession and their spiritual vitality. Our shared life together truly should overflow in a shared-out life that touches those both within and outside the faith community.

True *koinōnia* will not develop if members of the community only face inward and share life with each other. Such a community will grow insular and eventually will "starve" to death. Reaching out together is the only way to develop true vital community. In reflecting on the needs of the world, Elizabeth O'Connor asserted, "Unless a group of persons reach beyond themselves to touch and be touched by some of this need, its members will not know community."[10]

Conventional wisdom suggests that if we gather a group together for fun, fellowship, and spiritual nurture, a shared-out, missional attitude will develop naturally as people draw closer to one another in the group. Michael Frost, a teacher, writer, and evangelist from Australia, has noted that this in fact does not happen. A community founded solely to serve its members as an end unto itself will not last.[11] Conversely, community that grows out of a commitment to a greater mission will endure. Those who have participated in Work and Witness trips or local service projects often exclaim, "I think we (the team) got as much out of this as the people we went to serve" and "I can't believe how close we have become as a team!"

The shared-out attitude as we share life with those beyond the church nurtures and nourishes the fellowship of shared life within the church. The young adults in the Life Group mentioned earlier in this chapter have sought avenues of service to each other and to those outside the group since their very beginning as a group. They have provided meals for group members who have been hospitalized, baked cookies and delivered them to elderly members of the congregation, participated in work days at the local elementary school, and gathered clothing for homeless patients at a local hospital trauma center. Each time they serve together, they draw closer to each other as well.

CENTERED SET OR GATED COMMUNITY?

In North American society we have traditionally used the word "church" to refer to the building in which we gather as well as the people who gather there. This leads us to view the two as synonymous. To be part of the church (community) one must come to the church (building). "Come join us," we say.

Missionary anthropologist Paul Hiebert was the first to apply to the church the systems science concepts of "bounded set" and "centered set." Guder and his team have elaborated on this notion in their work on the missional church. A bounded set is a social organization or system with very clear boundaries, much like a housing development with metal gates at the entrance, accessible only to those who possess a key card or a code number. In a bounded set clear rules for belonging develop. One easily can detect who is in and who is out of the system. Once inside the bounded-set system, members may or may not clearly identify their focus (or center), but they rest in knowing they belong to the group. Members tend to look and act like each other. In order to belong, newcomers who enter the system soon start to look and act like everyone else.

Conversely, a centered set has "fuzzy" boundaries; no clear lines exist at the perimeters to indicate belonging. Rather, the system is organized around a clear center, a focus toward which all participants in the group are oriented, toward and around which they move. Entry points are not clearly delineated.

Guder and his team suggest that denominations and congregations often have functioned to provide boundaries, forming bounded sets. They argue that current trends in our society have led to the erosion of those boundaries, creating confusion about what it means to belong. They envision, instead, moving toward the model of a missional covenant community (a bounded set), functioning within a centered-set congregation.[12] The center, or focus, of the church is the reign of God. The "centered-set congregation invites people onto a journey with Jesus in order to understand its contours, to hear its stories, to sort out the issues and questions of commitment and discipleship."[13] Throughout this journey, those in the centered-set congregation are called to move forward and commit to the practices and disciplines of the bounded-set covenant community. The covenant community is not closed or cut off from the rest of the congregation. It continues to invite others to participate and enter into covenant with them, functioning missionally within the centered set of the larger community. People can enter the covenant process as they see the way of Jesus and choose to follow him.

RESULTS OF *KOINŌNIA*

Koinōnia Shapes Us

As we, the church, live in true *koinōnia,* the community shapes us. We grow together, becoming more and more like Jesus as we serve God and serve each other in love. A reciprocal process develops in that we are formed or shaped *for* mission, yet we are also formed while *on* mission and *in* mission.

As we engage in God's mission together, we learn how to live lives worthy of our calling as God's children. David Augsburger described *koinōnia* as "not just a peak experience of 'fellow-feeling'; it has continuity, a stubborn loyalty that endures. In this profound fellowship of life lived in relationship, the individual self is surrendered and then regained transformed, yielded in its individualism but rediscovered with rich individuality."[14]

Koinōnia Brings Reconciliation

"How very good and pleasant it is when kindred live together in unity!" (Ps. 133:1). As we share life together in community and conform more closely to the image of God, healing and reconciliation occur in us as individuals and as a community. The Greek verb *therapeuein,* from which we derive "therapy" and "therapeutic," means to serve or to take care of. We act as a therapeutic, healing community as we serve and care for each other and for the world around us.

David Augsburger has stated that in *koinōnia* we participate in the "kin-dom" of God where grace transforms human interaction:

The kin-dom of God grows among people as they join together in viewing one another in a radically new perspective—seeing each other as God sees us in grace—and then treating each other accordingly. Within this new kin-dom, followers of Christ participate in the social construction of an alternate reality. In place of the vengeful, violent reality based on retaliation and retribution, they construct a world by the words and actions of forgiveness, restoration and reconciliation.[15]

Koinōnia Reflects God

As we share life together, we have the privilege of showing the rest of the world what life looks like under the reign of God. In our daily interactions with each other in the church and in our grace-filled outreach to those beyond the church, we bear witness to the gospel, the good news.

For this reason, Newbigin described the local congregation as "the hermeneutic of the gospel,"[16] that is, the means through which the rest of the world understands the gospel. We represent God to the world.

We live together, then—if we are living missionally—in the *koinōnia* fellowship of the Holy Spirit. Paul prayed for the church in every age: "May the grace of the Lord Jesus Christ, and the love of God, and the fellowship of the Holy Spirit be with you all" (2 Cor. 13:14, NIV).

Amen! May it be so, Lord.

17
COMPASSION
BEING THE HANDS AND FEET OF GOD
Harold E. Raser

Compassion is at the very heart of God's work in the world. Relieving suffering and freeing the oppressed are priorities with God. These, then, also are the priorities of the people of God, God's hands and feet in the world. We are to seek out the needy and suffering, offering them relief in the name of our compassionate God.

COMPASSION IN SCRIPTURE

Christians recognize Jesus as the fullest revelation of God in the world. Luke described Jesus' reason for being as compassion. At the beginning of his public ministry, Jesus declared, "The Spirit of the Lord is upon me, because he has anointed me to bring good news to the poor. He has sent me to proclaim release to the captives and recovery of sight to the blind, to let the oppressed go free, to proclaim the year of the Lord's favor" (Luke 4:18-19).* These words from Isaiah 61:1-2 refer to the time of God's Messiah ("anointed one") that, Jesus announced, now had arrived. Jesus identified his mission as the ministry of compassion described by Isaiah. All Scripture testifies that God's heart is a heart of compassion for those who suffer.

The Old Testament

At the outset of biblical history, God showed compassion on the first humans though they had earned God's wrath through their rebellion. Because they were self-conscious and ashamed of their nakedness,

---

*All Scripture quotations in this chapter are from the NRSV.

a consequence of their sin, "The Lord God made garments of skins for the man and for his wife, and clothed them" (Gen. 3:21).

God acted in compassion to free the Hebrews enslaved in Egypt, saying, "I have observed the misery of my people who are in Egypt . . . Indeed, I know their sufferings, and I have come down to deliver them" (Exod. 3:7-8). When Israel settled in the land of Canaan, God instructed them to act as God acts. They were to have compassion toward the "alien" and the "stranger" in their midst because they themselves once had been "strangers in the land of Egypt" (Deut. 10:18-19). In the most comprehensive commandment to act with compassion, which Jesus identified as foundational for "all the law and the prophets" (Matt. 22:40), God instructed Israel, "You shall love your neighbor as yourself: I am the Lord" (Lev. 19:18).

When God's people forgot the priorities God had given them and began to live selfish, greedy, and uncaring lives, God sent the prophets to remind them of their responsibilities. The prophetic books are filled with warnings and exhortations about the importance of showing compassion. For example, Isaiah addressed the temptation of religious people to get so wrapped up in rituals and forms that they neglect actually to *be* the hands and feet of God in the world; "even though you make many prayers, I will not listen; your hands are full of blood . . . cease to do evil, learn to do good; seek justice, rescue the oppressed, defend the orphan, plead for the widow" (Isa. 1:15-17).

The New Testament

The compassionate nature of God is on display everywhere in the New Testament. Jesus not only *declared* his ministry to be a ministry of compassion but also *demonstrated* this at every opportunity. He cleansed lepers, cast out demons, gave mobility to the paralyzed, restored defective limbs, gave sight to the blind, and even raised the dead. Matthew reported that "Jesus went about all the cities and villages, teaching in their synagogues, and proclaiming the good news of the kingdom, and curing every disease and every sickness" (9:35).

Many of the New Testament writings that reflect on Jesus' ministry highlight the compassionate nature of God, especially as expressed in the love God has for the world. Not only do we read, "God so loved the world that he gave his only Son" (John 3:16), but also, "God is love, and those who abide in love abide in God, and God abides in them" (1 John 4:16) and "Let us love, not in word or speech, but in truth and action" (1 John 3:18). These passages, and many others, underscore that God is a compassionate God who loves humanity immeasurably. God desires human beings to receive God's love and share it with others through acts of compassion and mercy.

So we don't miss the message, the last book of the Bible reaches its culmination with a glorious description of the end time when God will bring all things to their fulfillment. This is a picture of God's compassion fully triumphant over everything that opposes it and brings suffering to humanity. Our compassionate God "will wipe every tear from their eyes. Death will be no more" because "mourning and crying and pain will be no more." At that time God will be "making all things new" (Rev. 21:4-5).

COMPASSION IN CHURCH HISTORY

The earliest followers of Jesus understood that compassion is at the very heart of God's work in the world. Having been with Jesus, or taught by those who had been his first disciples, they hardly could have missed this great truth! Thus, the early Christian church attempted to meet human need wherever they found it.

The Early Church

Some Christians exercised the gift of healing as God enabled them, following in the footsteps of Jesus who cured "every disease and every sickness" (Matt. 9:35). Some Christians had the gift of hospitality and welcomed into their homes travelers and strangers. Some visited those in prison, acted as advocates on their behalf, and tried to alleviate their suffering in a time when imprisonment could place a person in horrifying conditions. Many early Christians took special care of widows and orphans, two of the weakest and most vulnerable groups in ancient society. They are often singled out in Scripture as precious in God's sight and thus deserving of the aid and protection of God's people.

Early Christians became so renowned as people of compassion that some historians believe this was a major reason the church expanded as rapidly as it did in the first centuries after Pentecost. Christians became known as loving people always ready to share with those in need, though in the earliest centuries most Christians did not have much themselves. People were drawn to communities of believers in Christ who lived so differently from the self-centered, uncaring ways of the world.

By the fourth and fifth centuries, the Christian church had become large, widespread, highly organized, and accepted by governing authorities everywhere. The period of secrecy and persecution was over; Christianity had become legal and public. The heads of Christian congregations ("presbyters," "bishops," and the like) were often among the most respected persons in their communities. In this period the church was able to manifest compassionate mission in extraordinary ways.

In the late fourth and early fifth centuries, so-called barbarians (Germanic tribes from Central and Eastern Europe) began to invade a weakening Roman Empire. Eventually these Germanic tribes overran most of the western regions of the empire, occupying the city of Rome in A.D. 410. This was an extremely dangerous and difficult time for people throughout the Roman world. In many instances, church leaders acted as "protectors" of the inhabitants of towns (including Rome) that came under attack. They negotiated with the invaders, persuaded them to treat their captives humanely, and in other ways attempted to minimize the suffering of innocent people. Church leaders also led efforts to secure food and other necessities for towns under attack or occupation. They organized clinics and hospitals for the wounded and sick, and aided in the burial of the dead. In these and other ways, Christians acted as the "hands and feet" of a compassionate God in a time of monumental crisis in the ancient world.

The Monastic Orders

Monasticism was another way Christians embraced their mission of compassion in the church's early centuries. Many imagine monasticism to be mainly about retreat and withdrawal from the world since monasteries and convents seclude monks and nuns behind high walls, away from everything that might distract them from the worship of God and the pursuit of personal holiness. An impulse toward withdrawal and separation does exist in Christian monasticism, but that is only part of the picture. The withdrawal ultimately is for the purpose of gaining the necessary resources to go into the world again to serve God, the church, and one's fellow human beings. Thus, monasticism always has produced remarkable works of service and compassion in Christianity.

For example, through much of Christian history monks were the church's chief missionaries, belying the idea that monasticism is mainly about retreat from the world. They carried Christianity across the world in times when travel was extremely difficult and life in an unfamiliar culture could be very dangerous. They did this because of love for God and love for their "neighbor" who might reside thousands of miles away.

In addition, monks and nuns, both at home and in those places where they took the gospel as missionaries, often used portions of their monastic buildings as inns for travelers. These provided refreshment and a safe haven in ages before the conveniences of modern road systems and chain motels. Often Christian monastics also provided medical care for the sick and injured. ("Hotel" and "hospital" both come from the same root.) As early as the Council of Nicaea (A.D. 325), the Christian church committed to building and operating a "hospital" in at least every town that had a resident "bishop" ("overseer" of other pastors). Since monasteries and convents readily provided skilled staff, these "hospitals" often were attached to monastic communities.

Monks and nuns also operated schools, and to this day many monastic orders are especially known for their commitment to education (e.g., Jesuits, Sisters of Charity). Generally, these schools attempted to serve poorer students along with the wealthy, putting education within reach of those on the lower rungs of the societal ladder. At times in history, monastery and convent schools provided the only formal education available. In these times knowledge was kept alive and passed along to future generations solely through the efforts of devoted Christian educators.

For hundreds of years monastics spearheaded the work of compassion in the Christian church. Besides missions, inns, hospitals, and schools, monastic communities fed the poor ("soup kitchens"), gave shelter to widows and orphans, taught people useful trades by which they could support themselves, and even taught farmers how to make their land more productive (as a result of what they had learned themselves, from experimenting on monastery and convent land). Monastics were outstanding examples to the whole church of how to be the hands and feet of a compassionate God in the world.

COMPASSION IN THE WESLEYAN/HOLINESS CHURCHES

Through much of history, the Christian church has been diligent about representing God in the world through ministries of compassion. However, at times the church has been distracted from this priority. One example is the British Isles in the eighteenth century, the beginning of the Industrial Revolution, when dramatic social and economic change overwhelmed all British institutions, including the Church of England. Tens of thousands of people almost overnight became "aliens" and "sojourners" in their own country by moving from rural villages into new factory towns and cities for the jobs that supposedly existed there. Some never found work and were forced to take up begging, prostitution, or stealing to survive. Many children worked in factories to help their families keep afloat. Coal mining, central to the new system of coal-fired factories, attracted many men and boys. An extremely dangerous occupation, mining also routinely maimed and killed. As debtors' numbers increased in the new industrial economy, many were thrown into prison until they, family members, or friends could pay off their debts.

John Wesley

John Wesley (1703–91) grew up in these times of rapid change and great need. Wesley, a minister in the Church of England throughout his adult life, was troubled by the church's near paralysis in the face of these changes. He considered the church's tendency to preoccupy itself with worship rituals and teaching morality to already "respectable" people to be a betrayal of the church's mission in the world. Wesley envisioned a spiritually revitalized church living out what he called "scriptural Christianity," defined as loving God with all one's heart and loving one's neighbor as oneself. To live this way was to fulfill God's command to be "perfect," Wesley's own concept of Christian perfection. Wesley also believed the most fundamental nature of God is holy love. Thus, to be "perfect" as God is "perfect" (Matt. 5:48) is first and foremost to be a person who always acts out of love as God does (the Wesleyan concept of "perfect love").

Besides preaching and teaching that believers need to experience the fullness of God's grace ("entire sanctification") to be perfected in love, Wesley insisted that true godly love always is expressed in concrete acts of compassion toward those in need. Compassion for the most needy became the hallmark of the Wesleyan movement in eighteenth-century Britain. While many Christians ran from the huge challenges tossed up by the rapid changes in British life, Wesley's "Methodists," few in number and extremely limited in resources, organized numerous ministries of compassion.

A chief Methodist ministry was prison visitation. Since the poor were jailed for the smallest offenses, jails and prisons were crowded with poor people who could not afford to buy their way out of trouble. John Wesley, his brother Charles, and some of their friends made visitation of prisoners a priority from their days as students at Oxford. This continued as a mark of Methodism. Methodists even were known to climb into the carts taking condemned prisoners to their deaths, singing and praying with them, offering support in their last moments on earth. Wardens sometimes resented this "interference" and tried to banish them, but the Methodists became skilled at cultivating the support of sheriffs and others in authority who came to appreciate their compassionate work.

Methodists also became zealous educators. Their prison visitation convinced them that many people ended up in prison because they had no education; lives of petty crime and violence were one predictable result. John Wesley understood that a solid Christian education could help young people avoid such an end and live productive, Christian lives. Methodists built and operated schools all over the British Isles. Wesley himself founded schools at Bristol and Kingswood. These schools generally educated students of all ages and often provided clothing and food along with instruction.

Wesley established a system among his societies for supporting the various Methodist ministries of compassion. Each week society members contributed a penny to a fund for relief of the poor and sick. They also brought any clothing they could spare to be distributed among the needy.

Wesley organized a cottage knitting industry for women who needed work. He also appointed visitors to the sick. These visitors provided company for shut-ins, procured medicines, helped with household chores, and comforted the dying.

Wesley was so concerned with the physical well-being of his followers and others that he wrote *The Primitive Physik* (1747). In this home-remedy guide, he collected traditional treatments for various ailments and rated the usefulness of those he personally had tried. Wesley also coined the phrase "Cleanliness is next to godliness," emphasizing the fact that clean surroundings were less likely to breed disease. On this score Wesley was decades ahead of the professional medical community.

John Wesley's Methodist movement spread throughout the British Isles and to various other parts of the world, including North America. Everywhere the Methodists went they took with them their commitment to ministries of compassion, expressing in concrete ways the love of neighbor that reflects the love of God for the world.

THE HOLINESS MOVEMENT

Like most religious movements, as Methodism expanded it became preoccupied with growth, with organizational machinery and, increasingly, with "respectability." Compassion for the poor fell by the wayside (as did the doctrine of Christian perfection, which had fueled the Methodist emphasis on showing love for neighbor through concrete acts of compassion). In response to these changes, the holiness movement sprang up in the United States in the mid-nineteenth century. Its proponents hoped to inspire in Methodism a return to the "old paths," that is, to the priorities and practices that had characterized early Methodism.

The holiness movement, from its first stirrings in the preaching of the American Methodist laywoman Phoebe Palmer (1807-74), emphasized the original, biblical, Methodist priority of compassionate love for the poor, the marginalized, and the vulnerable. Palmer herself invested extraordinary amounts of time and energy in ministries of compassion. A partial list of her involvements includes: prison visitation; secretary of the Female Assistance Society; the Five Points Mission and a sister manufacturing enterprise, Five Points House of Industry; and the "Home for the Friendless" for orphaned children.

Phoebe Palmer's emphasis on expressing love to neighbor through acts of compassion and mercy marked the holiness movement as it gained popularity throughout the nineteenth century. When the movement produced independent holiness churches in the post-Civil War era, these churches faithfully reflected the Wesleyan heritage of compassion. Some founded rescue missions to minister to the homeless. Many congregations maintained food pantries, clothing closets, and "Good Samaritan funds" for those in need. Some even provided legal advice and representation or supported basic health care clinics.

At the beginning of the twentieth century, holiness Christians were appalled by society's toleration of prostitution, by its often callous treatment of "fallen women," and by the lack of care for the children of unwed mothers. Early-twentieth-century America considered sexual activity on the part of unmarried women beyond the pale. (That we read "women" here and not "men" also is the definition of the infamous double standard.) Unmarried pregnant girls often were ostracized, thrown out of their homes without help or support. Rescue homes (or rest cottages) operated by holiness churches were safe and healthy havens during pregnancy, through childbirth, and beyond.

Holiness groups usually operated orphanages with rescue homes, providing shelter for children of unwed mothers and facilitating their adoption by "good families." Often the rescue home/orphanage complex included a school, both for the young women and for their children. Vocational training gave the young women employable skills, helping them break out of the cycle of poverty that otherwise trapped them.

CONCLUSION

This brief survey has shown that compassion is at the heart of God's nature and of God's work in the world through God's people. Relieving suffering and freeing the oppressed are priorities with God. Through loving acts of compassion and mercy toward the neighbor in need, the people of God are God's hands and feet in the world—embodying God's nature and enacting God's will. Wherever and whenever the church is enlivened by God's Holy Spirit, faithfully seeking to follow the example of Jesus whose earthly ministry reveals to us the compassionate heart of the Father, the people of God will be a people of compassion.

Compassion is central to God's heart

18
WITNESSES OF GOD'S GRACE
Lyle Pointer

◆

Several Ethiopians sat on the church lawn between worship and Sunday school, smoking cigarettes and eating while they told stories and laughed. First-time visitors to that congregation drove by the building and saw the "unofficial" greeters. They drove on.

This prospective family phoned the church office later that week. "We drove by the church on Sunday morning and were surprised to see black people outside the entrance."

"We are a multicultural congregation," the pastor responded, "with services conducted in four languages. Our English-speaking congregation has Japanese, Chinese, Filipinos, African-Americans, . . . even Texans!" He chuckled at his attempt to use a joke to soften the conversation.

The caller ignored the humor. "Oh. We're looking for something else."

When the pastor recounted the story for the church board, the board members promptly confirmed that they wanted to be the kind of congregation where anyone felt accepted.

Jesus lived out the mission of God that way. In Jesus' time, for example, women were pushed to the margins of society. One day in Samaria Jesus met a woman who had come to draw water from the town well. He engaged the woman in conversation by asking if she would supply him with a drink. She was shocked that a man—a Jewish man at that—would even speak to her. Intrigued by his willingness to reach across the social divide and tantalized with the idea that this stranger would ask her for a favor, the woman began to debate with Jesus. Before long, Jesus offered the woman water that would fully satisfy. The more she listened to Jesus the more evidence she saw that he was the Messiah. She could not contain the good news and ran into town to announce the arrival of Jesus, the one anointed by God. Many believed in the Savior because of her testimony.

Shocked by Jesus' counter-cultural behavior

(against societal norm)

In Jesus' teaching, stories, and actions we clearly see God's desire that all persons would choose holiness over a life of sin. In John 3:16 Jesus declared God's purpose of saving perishing people because of God's love for the world. When a religious group scoffed at Jesus for spending time with sinners, Jesus launched into a story about a lost sheep. The shepherd left the ninety-nine to search for the one lost sheep. A corner of heaven was pulled back to show the great rejoicing for the lost that now was found. At a time when Jesus' popularity could have drawn him like a magnet to those already excited by his presence, Jesus said, "Let us go somewhere else—to the nearby villages—so I can preach there also. That is why I have come" (Mark 1:38).* Jesus' actions embodied his teaching that God reaches out to draw all persons into the community of faith.

When Jesus taught his disciples to pray, they learned that God desires a complete restoration of the earth and all that is in it: "Your kingdom come. Your will be done, on earth as it is in heaven" (Matt. 6:10). Heaven's standards are overlaid on human activity. God has given us the ambassadorial ministry of reconciliation (2 Cor. 5:18-20). We are to witness to the world that God's rule has begun.   *Reconciliation*

The good news is that God initiated the process. Wesleyans understand this as prevenient grace, God's love in action on our behalf preceding our salvation. God already is at work, even before any individual or organization gets involved. God graciously draws all persons into relationship.

When the church participates in what God already has started, the church becomes a means of God's grace. The church by its very existence is witness to the redeeming love of God. That witness involves an incarnational presence, redemptive conversations, compassionate care, and an inclusive community.

THE WITNESS OF INCARNATIONAL PRESENCE

God calls the church to embody the gospel, to witness to God's reign through an incarnational presence. We find this in the church after Pentecost. In Acts 2:42-47, Luke described an energetic, joyful commu-

---

*All Scripture quotations in this chapter are from the TNIV, except as noted.

nity of Jesus' followers. People took notice when they saw how the Christians fellowshipped with each other, and liked what they saw. Dining was frequent and pleasant. Prayer, teaching, and worship established a daily rhythm. The church shared what they had with others who needed assistance. The witness of this grace-infused church attracted new people into their fellowship.

Just as it was for Jesus, the witness *lifestyle* of the early church was not an event or a program, but a 24/7 lifestyle. Jesus never practiced photocopy evangelism. To only one person did he say, "You must be born again" (John 3:3, 7). To some, he said, "Follow me and I will make you fish for people" (Mark 1:17, NRSV), while to others he said, "Repent, and believe in the good news" (Mark 1:15, NRSV). The first Easter Sunday, on the road to Emmaus, Jesus talked with two distraught followers whose spiritual conclusions were tentative and whose fears were great. With Thomas, a week later, Jesus offered his hands to wipe away the doubt. The examples Jesus provided show that witness to God's mission comes in the ongoing cadences of life, not in an occasional event, and that it assumes forms appropriate to each situation.

Bonnie lived that way too. She attended college and worked two jobs, a schedule that often left her weary. When she came to church, though, she rarely came alone. Sometimes a student she worked with as a part of her practicum would come with her. The next week she might bring her mother, sister, nephew, or aunt. Bonnie witnessed to the gospel in the everyday business of life. She constantly sought to care for people, and she linked her concern with her faith in Jesus as Savior.

Art needed some assistance, so he came to the church hoping we could help him. He quickly declared himself an agnostic. After we provided assistance and food, Art started hanging around a bit. He attended the morning worship service on occasion and even tried an adult Bible study fellowship. "Art," I asked, "why do you attend our church when you doubt there is a God?"

His answer encouraged me, "In the hope there is one." A debate might never convince someone like Art, but he paid attention to the witness of a congregation that embodied the gospel.

people PAY ATTENTION

The beginning of the Great Commission (Matt. 28:19a) literally reads, "Therefore, in your going [i.e., during the daily things you do] make disciples" (author's translation). Christian witness occurs day by day. Sometimes it is serendipitous, as God brings surprises into the day. Effective witnesses, however, also move intentionally into situations where people need God's grace: a woman volunteers at a hospice; a congregation adopts an elementary school in the neighborhood; regular mall walkers get to know each other. The attentive witness regularly looks for opportunities to be a means of grace.   *Alertness + Intentionality*

"In your going" remember God is already there. You don't have to initiate God's gracious invitation. Just allow your own presence to witness to the beauty of living under the reign of God.

THE WITNESS OF REDEMPTIVE CONVERSATIONS

The Christian witness, in addition to being present, engages in redemptive conversations. Contrary to the stereotype of a personal evangelist bursting in with all the right words, the effective witness begins a redemptive conversation by listening with interest, discernment, and sensitivity. Christian witnesses know God's prevenient grace is already at work, so they seek first to recognize God's nudges in another person's life.

The first thing some of us must do to listen well is . . . well: *stop talking.* Sounds simple enough, but for some, it takes discipline. Don't worry about filling the silent spots. Listen with your ears, yes, but also with your eyes and heart. What is your conversation partner saying in gestures and body language? What emotions saturate the words? Ask questions not to probe, but to clarify, then reflect back what you heard.

A missional congregation listens well in the community where they live. You can initiate conversations with the mayor and other city leaders, with public safety personnel such as police officers and fire responders, with educators, social workers, and medical personnel. Read your local newspaper with an eye toward discerning the people and places where God's grace is needed. Pay attention to the conversations you hear in coffee shops and health clubs, not to interfere, but to learn.

In listening to others, look for evidence of broken trust. Rick Richardson says, "In spiritual friendships with people who don't know Jesus,

Listen well.

assume mistrust [italics his], just as Jesus did. If we assume mistrust and seek to identify with broken trust and defuse it, we will discover unending opportunities for meaningful spiritual conversation."[1]

Betty, a woman in her sixties with leathery skin and a ready grin, visited our church. I asked if I could call on her and her husband. They agreed. Betty and Frenchy greeted me warmly when I entered their home. Before long, Frenchy started telling me of the mistreatment he had suffered through the years at the hands of professed Christians. He cited a handful of incidents where Christians had lied to him, had taken advantage of him in business dealings, or were sexually immoral. He gathered his anger into a sharp statement, "The church is full of hypocrites!"

Prompted by the Spirit, I asked, "Have you ever known anyone who lived the Christian life?"

Frenchy had a ready answer. "My dad really lived the godly life!" he said emphatically. "My dad was a Methodist minister, but the congregation he pastored was full of hypocrites. They mistreated him."

With that, the tears began to flow down Frenchy's cheeks. He waved me away with the back of his hand. I stood to my feet, thanked them for letting me visit, and started for the door. Betty put her arm in my arm and walked me to my car. She apologized for her husband's anger. I assured her it was a privilege to share his pain.

A couple of months later Frenchy showed up at church. His spiritual journey toward Jesus started because I listened to his story.

As you listen to the broken-trust stories of others—and to the Holy Spirit for discernment—you'll find a place where you can begin telling stories of God's transformative work in your life. Richardson wrote, "Then, as you have found common struggles and sufferings, needs and longings, you can speak of how your spiritual experiences and connection to God have helped you in the midst of your struggles. . . . Don't look for ways that you are stronger, better or more successful than your friend. Look for the similar struggles and hurts. And then talk from your heart about the difference closeness to God has made."[2]

look for SIMILARITY, x'honor"

THE WITNESS OF COMPASSIONATE CARE

The effective Christian witness is present, listens well, and compassionately cares for the friend.   *Be Present.*

George Hunter met with more than eighty groups over six years as part of a research project. He invited people who believed evangelism was important, but who were not personally doing the work of an evangelist, to talk with him. Hunter says that in those conversations he discovered what he classified as "the greatest barrier to evangelism in our churches."

When Hunter asked people *why* they were not doing evangelism, they usually responded with, "I am not that sort of person." So he probed to discover the kind of person whom they thought does evangelism. In response, they tended to use adjectives such as "dogmatic, holier-than-thou, narrow-minded, self-righteous, pushy, aggressive, overbearing, judgmental, hypocritical, insensitive, and fanatical." That's an unfortunate list, but it helps explain why people often do not want to be associated with evangelism.

By contrast, when Hunter asked those who recently had begun to believe on Jesus as their Savior to describe the persons who had influenced them to come to Christ, they used adjectives like "loving, caring, informed, understanding, accepting, affirming, interested, concerned, encouraging, supporting, kind, and credible." When Hunter pointed out the disparity between the lists, one Christian observed, "We have been duped into assuming that you cannot be like Jesus if you want to reach people for Jesus!"[3]

The compassion with which Jesus ministered to people should characterize also the witness of Jesus' followers to God's grace. James, discussing the integral linkage between faith and deeds, said, "I will show you my faith by what I do" (James 2:18b). Compassionate care demonstrating the gospel is a powerful witness. Todd Hunter has suggested, "A community of faith living in creative goodness on the behalf of others may be the most powerful demonstration of the gospel, the most effective form of evangelism in contemporary society."[4]

I received an e-mail from a gay couple wanting to worship with our congregation. The subject line read "Questions," and the message got right to the point, "Hello. I just have a couple of questions. I believe what the Bible says in regards to homosexuality, yet, I have lived with my partner for almost eight years and we desperately want to find a church home. I'd like to know how comfortable we would be attending your church. Do you have other gay people or gay couples in your congregation? Please respond when you can. One of us is ill and we both need to find peace. Kindly yours, Shannon."

I replied, "I regret you are ill. I am glad you desire peace. I do not know how comfortable you will be at our church, but I can assure you that you will be accepted. People will offer friendship and treat you with kindness. I do not know of other gay people. We care for all who want to fellowship with us. I look forward to meeting you."

Shannon attended a worship service shortly after the e-mail exchange and a few Sundays after that he brought his partner to church. That began a journey toward God that led Shannon to rededicate himself to Christ. The compassionate care the congregation showed Shannon made it easier for him to hear the Holy Spirit call him to repentance. What started as a fear of rejection came to the place where Shannon declared, "I have found my 'church home.'"[5]

A consistency between words and deeds intensifies the witness of the church as each reinforces the other. The message of God's love is to be seen in our love for people. Without the supporting relationships of good will and caring, the message of love becomes an unreal and lofty ideal. Because of God's love for us, we weave together words and actions as a beautiful witness of God's grace and mercy.

WITNESS OF THE INCLUSIVE COMMUNITY

The effective witness of the church, as it participates in what God has begun, involves being available through an incarnational presence, listening well as the first step in redemptive conversations, and matching words with deeds of compassionate care. All this emerges from a church community that eagerly receives any seeker of God.

Christian witness is the responsibility of the church, the community of faith, and not solely of individual Christians. Paul told the Ephesians that God's "intent was that now, through the church, the manifold wisdom of God should be made known to the rulers and authorities in the heavenly realms, according to his eternal purpose that he accomplished in Christ Jesus our Lord" (Eph. 3:10-11). We recognize that individuals do their part for the church to fulfill God's intent, but the responsibility to witness to God's grace lies on the shoulders of the congregation as a whole.

In *The Celtic Way of Evangelism,* George Hunter contrasted the Roman model for reaching people for Christ (followed by most evangelicals), with the Celtic model. In the Roman model, the evangelist presents the Christian message, invites the person to make a decision to believe in Jesus as Savior and, if the response is positive, invites the person into the fellowship of the church. By contrast, the Celtic model starts with bringing the person into fellowship with the community of faith. As part of the community, then, the person participates in the regular rhythms of the congregation. In time, the person comes to believe and makes a commitment to serve Christ through the church. Hunter's own research confirms the effectiveness of the Celtic model in today's world, "Many new believers report that the experience of the fellowship *enabled* [italics his] them to believe and to commit."[6]

Welcoming pre-Christians into the life of a congregation could happen beyond the church facility. Unchurched people are also moved by human need, so a congregation could invite unbelievers to join them in extending the grace of God in the community. Habitat for Humanity, for example, clearly identifies itself as a Christian housing ministry, but their volunteers include people outside, as well as those from within, Christian congregations. Christians motivated by the love of God become witnesses for Christ to those who work alongside them for the good of the broader community.

Many hospitals were started by church groups or by individual Christians. An example is The Children's Center, a pediatric hospital in Bethany, Oklahoma, founded in 1898 when Mattie Mallory felt God's call to help orphans. Just as Mattie welcomed abandoned children, so the church is to be known by its welcoming hospitality. The words "hospital" and "hospitality" have a common root, with a basic meaning of "to make room for" persons on the outside.

The apostle Paul had a high view of hospitality. Among the Christian's "lofty" pursuits, such as righteousness (Rom. 9:30) and love (1 Cor. 14:1), Paul included the pursuit of hospitality (Rom. 12:13). Paul urged Christians to be active in "making room" for others, to seek opportunities, intentionally, for inviting people into the fellowship of the saints. The witness of the church is effective, as people beyond the church find a warm welcome among the followers of Jesus.

SUMMARY

In recent years the practice of evangelism typically has been to approach an unsaved person on the basis of preparation for life after physical death, for getting ready for heaven. Obviously the gospel endorses such a message, but the goal of evangelism cannot be reduced to that one thing. When we pray the Lord's Prayer, we invite God's will to be done on earth as it is in heaven. While the first approach emphasizes urging people, "Get ready to die," the latter proclaims, "Hurry; start a love relationship with God and you really can live *now*!"

Our tendency may be to select one approach over the other, but as Christians with a high view of Scripture we embrace both. God is the God of eternal life, and eternal life is not relegated to the future; we can experience it abundantly right now. Such an understanding motivates the follower of Jesus to live in both faithfulness and fruitfulness. We do not sit passively waiting for the future life to arrive; rather, we join the divine effort to bring God's kingdom into this present world. We want others also to experience the fullness of God's life here and now.

Jesus *is* Lord. We do not have to usher in the reign of God, or keep the King on his throne. Our role is to witness to God's goodness and holiness as we embody the gospel in a life that participates in God's transforming work among us. The church is both witness to and participant in God's redemptive mission.

Actively witness + particip. in God's mission

19

BECOMING WHO WE ARE
FORMED FOR MISSION
Douglas S. Hardy

◆

"Houston, we've had a problem!" Apollo 13 Commander James Lovell said to Mission Control.[1] In April 1970, as a young boy living in Canada, I joined people around the world glued to their television and radio sets awaiting the fate of three American astronauts trying to make it back to Earth alive in a crippled spacecraft. A fault in the electrical system of the Apollo 13 service module produced an explosion, loss of electrical power, and failure of its oxygen tanks. A mission intended to include a third lunar landing for the NASA program had to be aborted.

The Apollo 13 astronauts and technicians were not the first, nor will they be the last, to encounter a problem in carrying out a mission. Any missional venture, even the mission of God, can encounter problems that sidetrack, if not threaten, the success of the mission.

"Wait a minute!" you may be thinking. "How could *God's* mission *ever* be in jeopardy?" While we may be tempted to assert that anything associated with God is guaranteed to succeed, the Scriptures as well as centuries of religious history tell us differently.

To be sure, God's missional presence, in the person of the Holy Spirit, will continue in our world, and ultimately God will accomplish God's desires for the world. This we can count on. But because God has linked God's mission with human beings, the mission will be more or less present and powerful at any given time, depending on the quality of our relationships and participation with God in this mission. God expresses God's purposes in and through human beings and human communities. Herein lies the potential for, as well as the problem with being, missional.

THE POTENTIAL:
FORMED AT THE CREATION OF THE WORLD

When we consider our participation with God in God's mission, the appropriate beginning place is the scriptural record of our beginnings, the Genesis account of creation. We know God to be a missional God because "in the beginning God created" (Gen. 1:1, NIV). God extended beyond Godself to create and then interact with that creation, seeking its welfare and sustaining its life. To say God is missional is to say God creates, gives shape, forms.

What, then, is *our* basis for being missional? It is being on the receiving end of that same relationship. We are missional to the extent we are dynamically in relation with the missional God. The missional God creates; we are *created*. The missional God gives shape; we are *shaped.* The missional God forms; we are *formed*; "The Lord God formed man from the dust of the ground" (Gen. 2:7).*

The most ground-level (literally!) basis for our being missional is being in relationship with God, but not just any kind of relationship. It is a formational—a created, shaped, dynamic—relationship. We are missional when we are being formed by the missional God whose signature act is forming.

A right understanding on this is important. I am not missional simply because I state God's mission. I am not missional simply because I have a desire to participate in God's mission. I am not missional simply because I do things that can be labeled missional. No. I am missional, first, because I am in dynamic relationship with the missional God who formed me. I am missional, first, because I was formed for mission.

In what ways were we formed for mission at the creation of the world? The first two chapters of Genesis provide a rich description of God's work of formation. Amid this richness a simple pattern emerges: God formed by taking what was already present (void, darkness, water, ground), infusing God's desire for something other than what already was (wind, spirit, breath), and thereby freely creating new life (light, goodness, being).

---

*All Scripture quotations in this chapter are from the NRSV, except as noted.

What is already present	+	Desire for an "other"	=	Conditions for new life

This pattern describes what we mean when we say "God is love" (1 John 4:16). True love, God shows us, is giving oneself for the sake of the life of an "other"—someone not me and not even like me. We were formed by this kind of love. God formed us with a vital connection to the stuff around us (ground), a vital connection to the God who made us (spirit), and a way of being with God and the rest of creation that helped (and helps) further the emergence of and care for new life.

Because of how we were formed—"God created humankind in his image" (Gen. 1:27)—our inaugural mission was a clear reflection of God's mission. We were to "be fruitful and multiply, and fill the earth and subdue it" (v. 28); we were to "till the ground" (2:5) and "keep" the garden (v. 15).

Formed in God's image, we had the capacity to participate in God's mission of choosing to love others into being—plants, animals, and fellow human beings. As Genesis 3 makes clear, however, this capacity to participate in God's mission entailed the possibility of failure. And fail we did. The amazing potential for a missional humanity benefiting the entire creation was not fully realized. We who were *formed* at the creation of the world were also *deformed* while living in this same world.

THE PROBLEM: *DE*-FORMED WHILE LIVING IN THE WORLD

The Christian version of the famous Apollo 13 transmission would sound something like, "Church, we've had a problem!" *This* problem has been around for a long time. In the tragic story of Genesis 3, sin entered the world, de-forming what God had formed. The great potential for missional partnership with the missional God came undone, dramatically evidenced in the garden disobedience of Adam and Eve, and then in their son Cain's murder of his brother, their other son, Abel. The mission of nurturing life was hijacked by the taking of life (Gen. 4:8).

How quickly and how extensively things fell apart! Perhaps this is not surprising, however, in light of the new pattern that emerged—the distortion of God's original pattern for the work of formation. Like God, the first humans took what was already present (God's word, knowledge, the stuff of the earth). Unlike God, however, they infused a desire for extending themselves (more knowledge, approval, standing, goods, pleasure, power), instead of a desire—God's desire—for others.

This distortion led to using others for one's own purposes, a strategy that ultimately fosters death (enmity, violence, alienation, domination).

distortion

What is already present	+	Desire for extending me/us	=	Conditions for death

The consequences of this new pattern are evident as the Genesis story unfolds: fear and hiding (3:10), shifting of blame (vv. 12-13), eviction (vv. 23-24), murder (4:8), homelessness (vv. 11-14), "taking" wives (v. 19; 6:1-2).

This distorted pattern is not unique to Adam and Eve and their immediate descendants. It signals the characteristic ways in which all humanity is deformed, that is, redirected from how we originally were formed for participating in God's mission. These deformations do not simply or easily disappear when one is in relationship with God through Jesus Christ, and becomes a part of the church. Otherwise, we could write off this whole discussion as applying only to non-Christians, to those outside the church, saying, in effect, "Houston, *they've* had a problem!"

No, church, *we've* had a problem. These deformations are so ingrained that they persist in the lives of Christian believers, evidenced in many of the practices of Christian communities. Remember, most of the stern words of correction in the New Testament are directed to followers of Jesus (see, e.g., Heb. 3:12).

The apostle Paul declared to an early Christian community, "I am astonished that you are so quickly deserting the one who called you in the grace of Christ and are turning to a different gospel" (Gal. 1:6). Paul's exasperation was justified. These deformations in the lives of believers and in Christian communities were not simply imperfections or human weaknesses that they needed to accept and to which they needed to adapt. No; these *de*formations were forming them in a gospel other than the gospel of Jesus Christ, sabotaging their capacity to be missional.

So it is with us. When our desire to extend ourselves ultimately shapes what we do with what we already have, we practice "another gospel" and severely limit our participation in God's mission.

In churches, this can take the form of setting goals to gain more members or stakeholders (extend our numbers), establish more churches in more places (extend our franchise), update our buildings and technological infrastructure (extend our relevance), or raise more money (extend our power and influence). These may be worthy goals, but to accomplish them, we do not have to be missional. We do not have to love as God loves. We do not have to encounter the "otherness" of others. We do not have to foster the conditions for something new to emerge. Consequently, too many communities of faith achieve their goal-centric agendas without godly formational qualities—without being formed by God and the gospel of Jesus Christ.   *goals & agendas w/o purpose*

Desire for more of what we already have, that is, extending our power, possessions, and prestige, is lust, not love. Lust of any stripe fuels using others for one's own ends, quenching life instead of nurturing the emergence of new life.

Love asks, "What is God already doing there, and how can I freely give (let go) so the emergence of new life is encouraged?" Lust asks, "What has God done here, and how can I control it, replicate it, multiply it, so I have (or at least am associated with) more of this life I know?" Lust in the church certainly includes consuming pornography, and extra- or non-marital affairs, but it also manifests itself as churches branding, niche-ing, and franchising Christianity.

Lust is but one biblical example of a deformation that interferes with our participation in the mission for which God formed us (1 John 2:16). Others include gluttony, greed, envy, anger, sloth, and pride. As the centuries-old Christian tradition reminds us, these sins are "deadly" to followers of Jesus, as they undercut our capacity to participate in God's mission of bringing new life into being.

When we are deformed—that is, formed by lust, gluttony, greed, envy, anger, sloth, or pride, rather than by God's Spirit (Gal. 5:16-26)— we lose touch with the dynamic relationships that undergird God's mission in the world:

- Our relationship with God. We begin to misrepresent God, using the God-we-think-we-know to advance our own interests.
- Our relationships with diverse and different fellow human beings. We misunderstand, misrepresent, and misuse them to advance our own interests.
- Our relationships with the rest of creation. We fail to see the need for empathic relationship with it, and end up misunderstanding, misusing, or even destroying it to advance our own priorities.

[handwritten in margin: consequences]

As though this were not bad enough, a further dynamic comes into play. These deformations habituate in us thinking and actions that keep us from self-examination. Desensitization to others fosters desensitization to ourselves, so that much of the time we are not even aware we are being deformed. It is possible (as with many of the Pharisees in the Gospels, and with the apostle Paul before his conversion) that we believe we are acting righteously. Even when we sense that something in us may be wrong, or we are challenged by others, we quickly retreat into self-justifying (or community-justifying) modes that preserve the status quo.

If we are not being formed for mission, we cannot fully participate in the mission. Our deformed living cuts us off at the roots. We may have an understanding of God's mission and a desire to participate in it, but fall short of actually living it. Why? Because we do not have the capacity to put into practice what we say with our words.

This sobering news is not ultimately bad news. The gospel (good news) of Jesus Christ offers an amazing promise: God can increase our capacity for participating in God's mission by forming us again and again. We who were *formed at* the creation of the world, but who have been *de*formed *while* living in the world, can be *reformed* to enable living *for* the world.

[handwritten at bottom: Need for reformation]

THE PROMISE:
RE-FORMED TO ENABLE LIVING FOR THE WORLD

In Paul's words to a group of early Christians that "I am again in the pain of childbirth until Christ is formed in you" (Gal. 4:19), we find the promise held out to all God's people. The potential for mission-in-and-with-God, that has become a problem of mission-serving-self-and-us, can be restored in Jesus Christ.

Jesus, the Son of God, by his life, death, and resurrection fully participated in the mission of God. He embodied it. Like his heavenly Father, Jesus loved the world by taking it as it was, infusing it with God's desire for something other than what was, and freely offering himself, even to the point of death, so new life might emerge.

Jesus, then, is our hope for embodying the mission of God in our lives and communities. As Christ is formed in us, we are *re*formed for mission.

It is important to note at this point that Paul was writing to people already identified with Jesus, brothers and sisters in the faith (Gal. 1:11), members of Christian churches (v. 2). Though believers, they needed to be formed in Christ. Accepting Jesus, coming to know Jesus, asking Jesus into your heart—these are ways we describe the beginning of a personal relationship with God in Christ. Like the booster rocket that launched Apollo 13 into space, initial conversion sets us on course for God's mission. Apart from having Christ formed in us, however, this beginning will not result in the ongoing conversion necessary for full participation with God in God's mission.

How is Christ formed in us so that we are *re*formed for God's mission in and for the world? This entire volume is an attempt to answer this question. When, as believers in the triune God, and members in the church of Jesus Christ in the power of the Spirit, we participate in worship, discipleship, shared life, compassion, and witness, we are being *re*formed for mission.

More precisely, we are put in position to be *re*formed for mission, for this re-formation is not automatic, nor is it guaranteed simply by doing these things. Something must occur in and among us before, during, and after our participation in the practices. We must be open to be *re*formed.

Open. This is the posture of the missional God and must be our posture too. We are formed for mission when we willingly:

- Open our eyes to see God as God is, ourselves as we are, and others as they are
- Open our hearts to welcome God's *reforming* work in us, in others, and in our world
- Open our hands to serve God by serving others in love

Christ cannot be formed in us when we close our eyes, our hearts, or our hands. Closed persons and closed communities cannot participate in the mission of God, because who we are trumps what we do (or say we will do). Recall God's simple yet profound words of response when Moses asked for the name of the missional God, "God said to Moses, 'I AM WHO I AM.' . . . Thus you shall say to the Israelites, 'I AM has sent me to you'" (Exod. 3:14). God is who God is. Similarly, we are who we are. If who we are is not an accurate reflection of who God is, we will not be able to join God in doing what God does. As Paul reported even of Peter, we may be charged with "not acting consistently with the truth of the gospel" (Gal. 2:14).

THE POSTURE: BECOMING OPEN TO GOD'S *REFORMING* PRESENCE

The Wesleyan tradition offers many rich resources to help us engage in practices that form us for mission; several have been highlighted in earlier chapters of this book. As we come to a conclusion, I would draw our attention to a practice that speaks especially to the issue of openness—openness to be *reformed* again and again by God's transforming Holy Spirit. This foundational practice is the Wesleyan Covenant Renewal Service.

When John Wesley published his "Directions for Renewing Our Covenant with God" in 1780, it embodied the heart or core of spirituality as he understood it—total commitment of one's whole life to God. Wesley believed serious Christians—those followers of Jesus who wish their lives and actions to match their beliefs and intentions—would benefit from an annual service of reflection and dedication, inviting Christians to:

- View life in this world from God's eternal and blessed perspective (the potential for mission for which we were formed)
- Confess the sin that deforms us and our absolute need for God's mercy and grace (the problem for mission caused by *deformation*)
- Offer ourselves to God in Christ, who will receive and appoint us to our work (the promise for mission in our *reformation*)

This posture of radical openness to God for the sake of others is captured beautifully in a contemporary rendition of Wesley's Covenant Prayer:

> *I am no longer my own, but yours. Put me to what you will, rank me with whom you will; put me to doing, put me to suffering; let me be employed for you or laid aside for you, exalted for you or brought low for you; let me be full, let me be empty; let me have all things, let me have nothing; I freely and heartily yield all things to your pleasure and disposal. And now, O glorious and blessed God, Father, Son, and Holy Spirit, you are mine, and I am yours. So be it.*[2]

When we pray and live into this prayer, we find that, as in Apollo 13's dramatic but safe return to earth, the very problems that seem to sabotage the fulfilling of God's mission can lead us to discover the means of grace for becoming who we are in God.

NOTES

Preface

1. John Addison Dally, *Choosing the Kingdom: Missional Preaching for the Household of God* (Herndon, VA: Alban Institute, 2008), 10-11.

2. Ibid., 11.

3. Charles Wesley, "Come, Sinners, to the Gospel Feast" in *Wesley Hymns* (Kansas City: Lillenas Publishing Company, 1982), 2.

Chapter 1

1. *The Nazarene Manual 2005-2009* (Kansas City: Nazarene Publishing House, 2005), 185.

2. Michael Goheen, *As the Father Has Sent Me, I Am Sending You: J. E. Lesslie Newbigin's Missionary Ecclesiology* (Zoetermeer: Boekencentrum, 2000), 36.

3. Short Term Mission conference, Chicago, Illinois. July 2009.

4. Andrew J. Kirk, *What Is Mission?: Theological Explorations* (Minneapolis: Fortress Press, 2000), 30.

Chapter 3

1. Walter Brueggemann, *Reverberations of Faith: A Theological Handbook of Old Testament Themes* (Louisville, KY: Westminster/John Knox Press, 2002), 37.

2. Terence E. Fretheim, *Exodus*, in *Interpretation: A Bible Commentary for Teaching and Preaching* (Louisville, KY: John Knox Press, 1991), 212. (Italics are Fretheim's.)

Chapter 5

1. The phrase "the kingdom of God" or an equivalent occurs at least seventy times in the Synoptic Gospels (Matthew, Mark, and Luke), *not* counting the parallels between those gospels.

2. Only John 3:3, 5; 18:36 mention the kingdom.

3. R. T. France, "Kingdom of God," in *Dictionary for Theological Interpretation of the Bible*, ed. by Kevin J. Vanhoozer (Grand Rapids: Baker Academic, 2005), 420. (Italics are France's.)

4. This is the commonly accepted translation now, but many mid-twentieth-century New Testament scholars argued for the translation, "The kingdom of God has arrived."

5. A. M. Hunter, *Introducing New Testament Theology* (Philadelphia: Westminster Press, 1957), 31.

Chapter 6

1. "But now, apart from the Law, God's saving covenant faithfulness (or 'righteousness') stands revealed . . . the saving covenant faithfulness (or 'righteousness') of God revealed through the faithfulness of Jesus Christ to all those exercising believing allegiance."

2. Other saving benefits could be added to this list.

3. The effects of the saving benefits overlap and only make sense within the framework of *a group* of people. To give just one example, adoption into God's family is just that, adoption *into a family*. And becoming a part of God's household is impossible apart from reconciliation *both* to God *and* to others (Eph. 2:1-11).

4. E.g., 1 Cor. 1:9, 26; 7:18, 20; Gal. 1:6; Eph. 4:1.

5. In v. 7, Paul explicitly referred to "you all" becoming a *singular* model as a whole congregation (although he certainly expected each person to live an exemplary life).

6. This need not mean the Thessalonians were street preaching. But others surely would have asked them about changes in their public behavior. In such conversations, naming Jesus as Lord and telling of his faithfulness to God's mission would have called their culture's idolatry into question, provoking the hostility of some.

Chapter 7

1. Lesslie Newbigin probably was the first missiologist to relate mission to the doctrine of the Trinity, in his book *Trinitarian Doctrine for Today's Mission* (Exeter: Paternoster, 1988/Eugene, OR: Wipf and Stock, 2006). Newbigin was following the lead of Karl Barth; see David J. Bosch, *Transforming Mission* (Maryknoll, NY: Orbis, 2005), 390.

2. The NRSV translates "Advocate" at each of these places.

3. Gregory of Nazianzus, Oration 38:8, *Nicene and Post-Nicene Fathers,* Second Series, Vol. 7, 346.

4. See Basil of Caesarea, "On the Holy Spirit," 47, *Nicene and Post-Nicene Fathers,* Second Series, Vol. 8, 29.

Chapter 8

1. Lesslie Newbigin came to see the centrality of the cross through reading James Denney's commentary on Romans. (See Donald Le Roy Stults, *Grasping Truth and Reality: Lesslie Newbigin's Theology of Mission to the Western World* [Eugene, OR: Wipf and Stock, 2008], 10.)

Chapter 9

1. This phrase appears in the Orthodox liturgy celebrating Easter and in hymns.

Chapter 10

1. Emil Brunner, *The Word and the World* (London: Student Christian Movement Press, 1931), 108.

2. Albert C. Outler, "Do Methodists Have a Doctrine of the Church?" in *The Doctrine of the Church,* ed. Dow Kirkpatrick (Nashville: Abingdon Press, 1964), 27-28. For further discussion about Nazarene and Wesleyan ecclesiology, see Melvin E. Dieter and Daniel N. Berg, eds., *The Church: An Inquiry into Ecclesiology from a Biblical Theological Perspective* (Anderson, IN: Warner Press, 1972), especially Melvin E. Dieter's chapter, "The Concept of the Church in the Nineteenth-Century Holiness Revival," 263-95. See also Melvin E. Dieter, *The Holiness Revival of the Nineteenth Century,* 2nd ed. (Lanham, MD: Scarecrow Press, 1996).

3. Cf. Article XIII, "Of the Church," of the Articles of Religion in *The Discipline of the United Methodist Church,* and Article XI, "The Church," of the Articles of Faith in the *Manual of the Church of the Nazarene.*

4. The Church of the Nazarene was without an Article of Faith on "The Church" until it was voted on as the 16th Article of Faith at the General Assembly in 1989. As printed in the *Manual,* it was (and is) placed as Article XI of the Articles of Faith.

5. Alexander Schmemann, *For the Life of the World* (Crestwood, NY: St. Vladimir's Seminary Press, 1973).

6. In the earliest days of Christianity, the first Christians were those who were living in *the Way.*

7. *The Works of John Wesley,* Vol. 7, *A Collection of Hymns for the Use of the People Called Methodists,* Franz Hilderbrandt and Oliver A. Beckerlegge, eds. (Nashville: Abingdon Press, 1983), 7:250-52. The phrase, "Thy nature and thy name is love," is taken from Charles Wesley's hymn "Wrestling Jacob."

8. Schmemann, *For the Life of the World.*

9. Rev. Martin L. Smith, former superior at the Society of St. John the Evangelist (SSJE) in Cambridge, Massachusetts, spoke those paraphrased words in a meditation on "Christ's Last Words" (n.d.), on a Good Friday at Trinity Church of Boston.

10. Nikos A. Nissiotis, "Pneumatological Christology as a Presupposition of Ecclesiology," in *Oecumenica: An Annual Symposium of Ecumenical Research* (Minneapolis: Augsburg Press, 1967), 235-52. A "Spirit-Christology" is an underlying assumption at work in this essay. Alongside Nissiotis' work, I have found Ralph Del Colle and Eugene F. Rogers to be extremely helpful. See Ralph Del Colle, *Christ and the Spirit: Spirit-Christology in Trinitarian Perspective* (Oxford: Oxford University Press, 1994). His statement, "Spirit-Christology is after all a model that exegetes the divine economy. The risen Christ cannot be understood to be the 'sender' of the Spirit if the incarnate Christ is not already the 'bearer' of the Spirit" (29), is especially insightful; see also Eugene F. Rogers, *After the Spirit: A Constructive Pneumatology from Resources outside the Modern West* (Grand Rapids: Eerdmans, 2005).

Chapter 11

1. Personal communication (2006) from the Rev. Mr. Simon Pierre, district superintendent of the Church of the Nazarene in Rwanda.

2. Personal communication (2009) from Julie Hathcock, Spencer's mother.

Chapter 13

1. Charles H. Kraft, *Anthropology for Christian Witness* (Maryknoll, NY: Orbis Books, 1996), 47-48.

2. The outline for these sections on gospel and culture came out of a conversation with Darrell Whiteman, formerly professor of Cultural Anthropology at Asbury Theological Seminary and now a vice president and resident missiologist at The Mission Society, Norcross, Georgia.

3. George G. Hunter III, *The Celtic Way of Evangelism: How Christianity Can Reach the West . . . Again* (Nashville: Abingdon Press, 2000), 20-23.

4. Andrew F. Walls, *The Cross-Cultural Process in Christian History* (Maryknoll, NY: Orbis Books, 2002), 30.

5. Abridged, with permission, from Keith Schwarz, "Uncommon Relationships," http://gappartners.org/index.php?option=com_content&task=view&id=37&Itemid=33 (accessed December 1, 2009).

Chapter 14

1. N. T. Wright, "Freedom and Framework, Spirit and Truth: Recovering Biblical Worship," *Studia Liturgica* 32 (2002), 193.

2. Ibid.

3. Stanley Hauerwas, "Worship, Evangelism, Ethics: On Eliminating the 'And,'" in *The Study of Evangelism: Exploring a Missional Practice of the Church,* eds. Paul W. Chilcote and Laceye C. Warner (Grand Rapids: Eerdmans, 2008), 212.

4. Robert E. Webber, *Journey to Jesus: The Worship, Evangelism, and Nurture Mission of the Church* (Nashville: Abingdon Press, 2001), 47.

5. Thomas H. Schattauer, "Liturgical Assembly as Locus of Mission," in *Inside Out: Worship in an Age of Mission,* ed. Thomas H. Schattauer (Minneapolis: Fortress Press, 1999), 3.

6. Darrell L. Guder, "Missional Structures: The Particular Community" in *Missional Church: A Vision for the Sending of the Church in North America,* ed. Darrell L. Guder (Grand Rapids: Eerdmans, 1998), 243.

7. Lesslie Newbigin, *The Gospel in a Pluralist Society* (Grand Rapids: Eerdmans, 1989), 151.

8. Sally Morgenthaler, "Planning Worship the Way We've Never Done It Before," in *Taking Risks in Ministry,* ed. Dale Galloway (Kansas City: Beacon Hill Press of Kansas City, 2003), 73.

9. For example, see Robert E. Webber, *Worship Old and New,* rev. ed. (Grand Rapids: Zondervan, 1994), 149-52.

10. See Clayton J. Schmit, *Sent and Gathered: A Worship Manual for the Missional Church* (Grand Rapids: Baker Academic, 2009), chapter 2, for a fuller discussion of the theological rationale for the structure of worship.

11. Robert E. Webber, *Ancient-Future Worship: Proclaiming and Enacting God's Narrative* (Grand Rapids: Baker Books, 2008), 91.

12. Newbigin, *Gospel in a Pluralist Society,* 151.

13. Rodney Clapp, *A Peculiar People: The Church as Culture in a Post-Christian Society* (Downers Grove, IL: InterVarsity Press, 1996), 116.

14. Morgenthaler, "Planning Worship," 70.

15. Sally Morgenthaler, "Worship as Evangelism," *REV!* (May/June 2007), 52.

16. "The Means of Grace," Sermon 16 in *The Sermons of John Wesley,* 1872, Thomas Jackson, ed., http://wesley.nnu.edu/john_wesley/sermons/016.htm (accessed September 14, 2009).

17. András Lovas, "Mission-shaped Liturgy," *International Review of Mission* 95 (July 2006), 355.

Chapter 15

1. Dean G. Blevins and Mark A. Maddix, *Discovering Discipleship: The Dynamics of Christian Education* (Kansas City: Beacon Hill Press of Kansas City, 2010).

2. Adapted from Lois Y. Barrett, ed., *Treasure in Clay Jars: Patterns of Missional Faithfulness* (Grand Rapids: Eerdmans, 2004), 159-72.

3. John Westerhoff, "The Challenge: Understanding the Problem of Faithfulness," in *A Faithful Church: Issues in the History of Catechesis,* eds. John H. Westerhoff III and O. C. Edwards Jr. (Wilton, CT: Morehouse-Barlow Co., 1981), 1-4.

4. Leonel L. Mitchell, "The Development of Catechesis in the Third and Fourth Centuries: Hippolytus to Augustine," in Westerhoff and Edwards, *A Faithful Church,* 51.

5. William Harmless, *Augustine and the Catechumenate* (Collegeville, MN: Liturgical Press, 1995), 40-45.

6. Ibid., 156-80; Mitchell, "Development of Catechesis," 75.

7. Harmless, *Augustine and the Catechumenate,* 185-90.

8. James Riley Estep Jr., ed., Jonathan Hyungsoo Kim, Alvin Wallace Kuest, Mark Amos Maddix, *C.E.: The Heritage of Christian Education* (Joplin, MO: College Press, 2003), 6.2-6.6.

9. Harmless, *Augustine and the Catechumenate,* 244-96, 300-324.

10. Westerhoff, "The Challenge," 2.

11. Harmless, *Augustine and the Catechumenate,* 185.

12. Ibid., 223-24.

13. Ibid., 144-49.

14. Harmless, *Augustine and the Catechumenate,* 258; Richard P. Heitzenrater, *The Poor and the People Called Methodists* (Nashville: Abingdon Press, 2002).

15. Norma Cook Everist, *The Church as Learning Community* (Nashville: Abingdon Press, 2002), 252-89.

16. Harmless, *Augustine and the Catechumenate,* 312.

17. Ibid., 334.

18. Lesslie Newbigin, *The Gospel in a Pluralist Society* (Grand Rapids: Eerdmans, 1989), 229-31.

19. Dean G. Blevins, "Practicing the New Creation: Wesley's Eschatological Community Formed by the Means of Grace," *Asbury Theological Journal* 57, no. 2, and 58, no. 1 (Fall 2002/ Spring 2003), 81-104.

Chapter 16

1. Robert D. Putnam, *Bowling Alone: The Collapse and Revival of American Community* (New York: Simon and Schuster, 2000), 19.

2. Reuben Welch, *We Really Do Need Each Other: A Call to Community in the Church* (Nashville: Impact Books, 1973).

3. Stephen Seamands, *Ministry in the Image of God: The Trinitarian Shape of Christian Service* (Downers Grove, IL: InterVarsity Press, 2005), 35.

4. Darrell L. Guder, ed., *Missional Church: A Vision for the Sending of the Church in North America* (Grand Rapids: Eerdmans, 1998), 152.

5. Richard Lischer, *Open Secrets: A Memoir of Faith and Discovery* (New York: Doubleday, 2001), 211.

6. Elizabeth O'Connor, *The New Community* (New York: Harper and Row, 1976), 104, 106.

7. W. Ross Ashby, *An Introduction to Cybernetics* (London: Chapman and Hall, 1956).

8. Alan Hirsch, *The Forgotten Ways: Reactivating the Missional Church* (Grand Rapids: Brazos Press, 2006), 230.

9. Frank G. Carver, "The Second Epistle of Paul to the Corinthians," in *Beacon Bible Commentary: Romans, I and II Corinthians* (Kansas City: Beacon Hill Press of Kansas City, 1968), 588.

10. O'Connor, *New Community*, 10.

11. Michael Frost, *Exiles: Living Missionally in a Post-Christian Culture* (Peabody, MA: Hendrickson Publishers, 2006).

12. Guder, *Missional Church*, 201-20.

13. Ibid., 207.

14. David Augsburger, *Dissident Discipleship: A Spirituality of Self-Surrender, Love of God, and Love of Neighbor* (Grand Rapids: Brazos Press, 2006), 69.

15. Ibid., 70.

16. Lesslie Newbigin, *The Gospel in a Pluralist Society* (London: SPCK Publishing, 1989), 222-33.

Chapter 18

1. Rick Richardson, *Reimagining Evangelism: Inviting Friends on a Spiritual Journey* (Downers Grove, IL: InterVarsity Press, 2006), 76.

2. Ibid., 97.

3. George G. Hunter III, *The Apostolic Congregation: Church Growth Reconceived for a New Generation* (Nashville: Abingdon Press, 2009), 82.

4. Todd Hunter, *Christianity Beyond Belief: Following Jesus for the Sake of Others* (Downers Grove, IL: InterVarsity Press, 2009), 102.

5. Personal communications, used with permission; name changed to protect privacy.

6. George G. Hunter III, *The Celtic Way of Evangelism: How Christianity Can Reach the West . . . Again* (Nashville: Abingdon Press, 2000), 54.

Chapter 19

1. "Detailed Chronology of Events Surrounding the Apollo 13 Accident," NASA, http://history.nasa.gov/Timeline/apollo13chron.html (accessed December 13, 2010).

2. Frank Whaling, ed., *John and Charles Wesley: Selected Writings and Hymns* (New York: Paulist Press, 1981), 387.